LE-DAVID MASKIL

BIBLICAL AND JUDAIC STUDIES FROM THE UNIVERSITY OF CALIFORNIA, SAN DIEGO

Volume 9

edited by

William H. C. Propp

Previously published in the series:

1. *The Hebrew Bible and Its Interpreters*, edited by William Henry Propp, Baruch Halpern, and David Noel Freedman (1990).

2. *Studies in Hebrew and Aramaic Orthography*, by David Noel Freedman, A. Dean Forbes, and Francis I. Andersen (1992).

3. *Isaiah 46, 47, and 48: A New Literary-Critical Reading*, by Chris Franke (1994).

4. *The Book around Immanuel: Style and Structure in Isaiah 2–12*, by Andrew H. Bartelt (1996).

5. *The Structure of Psalms 93–100*, by David M. Howard Jr. (1997).

6. *Psalm 119: The Exaltation of Torah*, by David Noel Freedman (1999).

7. *Between Heaven and Earth: Divine Presence and Absence in the Book of Ezekiel*, by John F. Kutsko (2000)

8. *The Storm-God in the Ancient Near East*, by Alberto R. W. Green (2003)

LE-DAVID MASKIL
A Birthday Tribute for David Noel Freedman

Edited by
Richard Elliott Friedman
and
William H. C. Propp

EISENBRAUNS
Winona Lake, Indiana
2004

Published for Biblical and Judaic Studies
The University of California, San Diego
by
Eisenbrauns
Winona Lake, Indiana

Cataloging in Publication Data

Le-David maskil : a birthday tribute for David Noel Freedman / edited by
  Richard Elliott Friedman and William H. C. Propp.
       p.   cm. — (Biblical and Judaic studies ; v. 9)
  Includes bibliographical references and index.
  ISBN 1-57506-084-1
     1. Bible. O.T.—Criticism, interpretation, etc.   I. Freedman, David
  Noel, 1922–   II. Friedman, Richard Elliott.   III. Propp, William
  Henry.   IV. Series.
  BS1188.L42   2004
  221.6—dc22
                                                              2003024399

Contents

Introduction

May 12, 2002

Dear Noel,

We, your colleagues, wanted to give you a special gift for your eightieth birthday. And what could such a gift for David Noel Freedman possibly be but a book?! Now, we realize that you already have two *Festschriften*, containing, between them, about a hundred articles. But what can we do? You are quintessentially the man of the book. And perhaps what impresses us most is that your bibliography of hundreds of books is not limited to the extraordinary number of important books that you've written yourself. It also contains the books that you've edited for others. And we know what it means to have David Noel Freedman as one's editor. For every page of manuscript that the author sends you, you send back almost an equal number of pages of advice, criticism, corrections, and improvements. You can make a bad book good, and a good book better. And you can make its author a better scholar and a better writer.

So it had to be a book. The only thing we regret about this book is that it couldn't have you as its editor—but that would have spoiled the surprise! But we hope that it will bring you the satisfaction of knowing that your influence can be found in it: as our colleague, friend, and teacher, who has shared a great deal of wisdom with us over the years that you've been among us. And we hope that everyone who reads it and finds something of value in any of its chapters will know that it exists only because you came here and were the kind of colleague who inspired us to offer you this tribute.

So here it is: the gift for the scholar who has everything.

With affection and all best wishes on your eightieth birthday from your colleagues at the University of California, San Diego, and from your former students who are now colleagues in the field,

> Richard Elliott Friedman
> Jeffrey C. Geoghegan
> David Goodblatt
> Michael M. Homan
> Risa Levitt Kohn
> Thomas I. Levy
> William H. C. Propp

Abbreviations

General

LB	Late Bronze Age
LH	Laws of Hammurapi
LXX	Septuagint
MT	Masoretic Text
JB	Jerusalem Bible
JPSV	Jewish Publication Society Version
KJV	King James Version
NEB	New English Bible
NJPSV	New Jewish Publication Society Version
NKJV	New King James Version
NRSV	New Revised Standard Version
RSV	Revised Standard Version
OB	Old Babylonian

Reference Works

AB	Anchor Bible
ABD	*The Anchor Bible Dictionary.* Edited by D. N. Freedman. 6 vols. Garden City, N.Y.: Doubleday, 1992
AbrNSup	Abr-Nahrain Supplements
AfO	*Archiv für Orientforschung*
AHw	*Akkadisches Handwörterbuch.* W. von Soden. 3 vols. Wiesbaden: Harrassowitz, 1965–81
ANEP	*The Ancient Near East in Pictures Relating to the Old Testament.* Edited by J. B. Pritchard. Princeton: Princeton University Press, 1954
ANET	*Ancient Near Eastern Texts Relating to the Old Testament.* Edited by J. B. Pritchard. 3rd ed. Princeton: Princeton University Press, 1969
BA	*Biblical Archaeologist*
BAR	*Biblical Archaeology Review*
BARead	*Biblical Archaeologist Reader*
B.A.R. Int. Series	British Archaeological Reports, International Series
BASOR	*Bulletin of the American Schools of Oriental Research*
BDB	Brown, F., S. R. Driver, and C. A. Briggs. *Hebrew and English Lexicon of the Old Testament.* Oxford: Clarendon, 1907

BHS	*Biblia Hebraica Stuttgartensia.* Edited by K. Elliger and W. Rudolph. Stuttgart, 1983
Bib	*Biblica*
BR	*Bible Review*
BZAW	Beihefte zur Zeitschrift für die alttestamentliche Wissenschaft
CAD	*The Assyrian Dictionary of the Oriental Institute of the University of Chicago.* Edited by A. L. Oppenheim et al. Chicago, 1956–
CahRB	Cahiers de la Revue biblique
CBQ	*Catholic Biblical Quarterly*
COS	*The Context of Scripture.* Edited by W. W. Hallo. 3 vols. Leiden: Brill, 1997–
DJD	Discoveries in the Judaean Desert
EncMiq	*Encyclopedia Miqra'it.* 8 vols. Jerusalem: Bialik Institute
ER	*The Encyclopedia of Religion.* Edited by M. Eliade. 16 vols. New York: Macmillan, 1987
ErIsr	*Eretz-Israel*
HAR	*Hebrew Annual Review*
HSM	Harvard Semitic Monographs
HSS	Harvard Semitic Studies
HUCA	*Hebrew Union College Annual*
ICC	International Critical Commentary
IDB	*Interpreter's Dictionary of the Bible.* Edited by G. A. Buttrick. 4 vols. Nashville: Abingdon, 1962
IEJ	*Israel Exploration Journal*
IOS	*Israel Oriental Studies*
JANES	*Journal of the Ancient Near Eastern Society of Columbia University*
JAOS	*Journal of the American Oriental Society*
JAOSSup	Journal of the American Oriental Society Supplements
JARCE	*Journal of the American Research Center in Egypt*
JBL	*Journal of Biblical Literature*
JCS	*Journal of Cuneiform Studies*
JEA	*Journal of Egyptian Archaeology*
JJS	*Journal of Jewish Studies*
JQR	*Jewish Quarterly Review*
JSOTSUP	Journal for the Study of the Old Testament Supplement Series
JSPSup	Journal for the Study of the Pseudepigrapha Supplement Series
KTU	*Die keilalphabetischen Texte aus Ugarit.* Edited by M. Dietrich, O. Loretz, and J. Sanmartín. Alter Orient und Altes Testament 24/1. Neukirchen-Vluyn: Neukirchener Verlag, 1976
NEAEHL	*New Encyclopedia of Archaeological Excavations in the Holy Land.* Edited by E. Stern. 4 vols. Jerusalem: Israel Exploration Society, 1993
Or	*Orientalia*

PEQ	*Palestine Exploration Quarterly*
RB	*Revue biblique*
SBTS	Sources for Biblical and Theological Study
STDJ	Studies on the Texts from the Desert of Judah
TA	*Tel Aviv*
TWAT	*Theologisches Wörterbuch zum Alten Testament.* Edited by G. J. Botterweck and H. Ringgren. Stuttgart: Kohlhammer, 1973–2000
VT	*Vetus Testamentum*
VTSup	Supplements to Vetus Testamentum
ZA	*Zeitschrift für Assyriologie*
ZAW	*Zeitschrift für die alttestamentliche Wissenschaft*
ZDPV	*Zeitschrift des deutschen Palästina-Vereins*

Chapter 1
An Essay on Method

RICHARD ELLIOTT FRIEDMAN

We are living in an age in which some key passages from the Bible have come to be fulfilled. The Bible's first commandment is "Be fruitful and multiply and fill the earth," and it appears to be the first commandment that humankind has carried out—for better or for worse. And the great closing philosophical point of the book of Ecclesiastes, "Of making many books there is no end," has come to pass in our day as well—also for better or for worse. One of the side effects of the book and article explosion is that, in the lifetimes of all of us in David Noel Freedman's generation and my own, it has become no longer possible to read everything in our field. And so it is no longer expected of us, when we publish our research, to have read everything on the subject we are discussing. One can even leave out some of the big pieces: major, classic works on one's subject. This has worked out nicely for writers with a postmodern agenda of disarray. The result is that there is rarely a feeling of consensus, much less a feeling of having found the truth, in most areas of our field. In a classic collection of essays on the state of the field forty years ago (*The Bible and the Ancient Near East*, edited by G. E. Wright), John Bright's characterization of the field at that juncture was not exactly a picture of consensus and unity of direction:

> The whole field is in a state of flux. It is moving, certainly, but it is not always easy to say in what direction. Sometimes it gives the impression that it is moving in several mutually canceling directions at once. Even upon major points there is often little unanimity to be observed. As a result, scarcely a single statement can be made about the state of the field that would not be subject to qualification.[1]

---

1. J. Bright, "Modern Study of Old Testament Literature," in *The Bible and the Ancient Near East: Essays in Honor of William Foxwell Albright* (ed. G. Ernest Wright; New York: Doubleday, 1961) 2.

He did not know the half of it. In Bright's day there was practically unanimity compared to the present. On one hand, lack of consensus is not necessarily a bad thing in itself. If it opens doors to creativity, trying out new possibilities, and discovering new things, that's great. But if it means that colleagues are ignoring evidence and arguments, not governing their work by any principles, and not following any known method of research, then, well, here we are: *tohû wabohû*. One result is that we hear comments such as: "the so-called assured results of past generations are now in doubt" and "no one accepts the documentary hypothesis anymore." But the truth is that, of the recent works that claim to have overturned that classic hypothesis, I cannot think of a single one that properly took into account the classic works and arguments for the hypothesis. Nor do they address major current works on their subject.

I submit that it is time to stop bemoaning the fact that there is so little consensus in our field and to bemoan instead that there is so little respect for method—to stop declaring that the field is in disarray and to start resenting the fact that many are not listening or responding to one other. We could also bemoan the fact that there is a diminishing respect for training and expertise. When biblical scholars who are not trained in epigraphy do epigraphy, when archaeologists who are not trained in biblical source criticism and historiography do source criticism and historiography, we are all in danger.

This is an essay on method. It is intended for colleagues but especially for graduate students—both our own students here at the University of California and students of the Hebrew Bible at other institutions. A book presented to David Noel Freedman as a birthday gift is a particularly appropriate place for an essay on method, because Noel has been possibly the greatest force for method in our field. Through his teaching and scholarship, but most of all through his editing, Noel has done more than anyone in the history of our field to help scholars become better scholars. Lesser editors rewrite. A great editor shows us how to make our writing better. Just look at the acknowledgment pages of the books that Noel has edited, and you will see an array of scholars from a variety of backgrounds paying tribute to him with gratitude.

Some years ago, Hugh Williamson and I edited a book on the future of our field as seen by several of the best scholars of our then-young generation.[2] The opening quotation that we placed above our introduction to the book was from Nietzsche. It said:

---

2. R. E. Friedman and H. G. M. Williamson (eds.), *The Future of Biblical Studies: The Hebrew Scriptures* (Semeia Studies; Atlanta: Scholars Press, 1987).

The methods, one must say it ten times, are what is essential, also what is most difficult, also what is for the longest time opposed by habits and laziness.

I am proud to say that many fine scholars of my generation have brought a new degree of methodological rigor to biblical studies. But, regrettably, this cannot be said for the field as a whole.

Method is, in largest part, about the handling of evidence. I have been supersensitive to matters of method ever since my high school days, when I had the good luck to have one of those teachers who make an impression that lasts one's whole life, Mrs. Genevieve Gillen, who taught public speaking and debate. The most important lesson in method I ever had was in her class. She asked us students what the purpose of evidence is in debating. We gave all the proper wrong answers: to back up your points, to prove your case, to win. She said: the purpose of evidence is to find out what is really going on—to get at the truth—and then your case flows out of that. You don't stake out your position first and then go looking for evidence and arguments to back it up. That is exactly backwards. You study the evidence to determine what the situation factually is; and that *is* your case.

Some scientists and scholars have learned this lesson from experience, some know it instinctively, and some never get it. This is striking at this particular moment in the life of our field. In the early stages of research on the Bible, there was less material evidence to go on, so our forerunners' arguments were more theoretical. As is commonly pointed out, the nineteenth-century models of the Bible's formation reflected the dominant theories of the day about social evolution. But more secure forms of evidence have arisen in recent decades. We have linguistic evidence, which is a more demonstrable, quantifiable means of determining when a text was written than dating the text on the basis of a theoretical model or on a concept of the way a writer of a particular period would have felt about monarchy or exile or monotheism. We have citation and allusion among biblical sources, which are more certain connectors of a string of texts than is our sense of a similarity of style among them. We are able to observe narrative flow. That is, we can separate texts that all bear the marks of the Priestly source of the Torah, and when we read them in order we find an almost unbroken narrative. The same can be done with JE. This mechanism likewise is more reliable than style for identifying common authorship of texts. I believe that the research on the biblical Tabernacle by my teacher Frank Cross, by Menahem Haran, by myself, and most recently by Michael Homan is another case of a surer fulcrum from which to identify and date texts than the older sorts of evidence.[3]

---

3. F. M. Cross, "The Priestly Tabernacle," *BA* 10 (1947) 45–68, reprinted in *BARead* 1 (1961) 201–28; idem, "The Priestly Tabernacle and the Temple of Solomon," *From Epic*

Establishing the historicity of the Tabernacle (on which more space is spent than any other subject in the Torah) enables us to find time and location for texts.

These new collections of evidence therefore have dual value: first, for their impact on the central model of the field and, second, methodologically. The refinement of tools and skills of language, archaeology, and comparative literature (of the ancient Near East), plus superior techniques in historical analysis have meant less evaluation of biblical texts on grounds of theoretical, speculative judgments of the points of view they express. That is, a text is not automatically exilic because it expresses guilt—or, for that matter, because it predicts exile. It is not automatically late because it expresses hope. It is not early because it is short. It is not early or late or Northern or Southern because it is (supposedly) antimonarchic. This mode of argument persists, to be sure, but these more secure forms of evidence are undermining it.

Also of methodological interest: the argument that the manner of composition of the Hebrew Bible, as conceived in the documentary hypothesis, is without parallel in other ancient literature has finally been laid to rest. A collection of studies by Tigay et al. provided a number of comparative studies that should belie this objection. Ignoring the idosyncratic in literature, it was never a substantial argument in any case, and it will not be missed.[4]

Some of the methodological gaps that particularly pervade analyses of literary artistry in the Bible can be attributed to the fact that much of the impetus in artistry studies has come from individuals who were scholars of other literatures, not biblical scholars by training, and who therefore were not equipped to take on some of these avenues of scholarship, though they contributed valuable insights.[5] And at the reverse end of the spectrum, biblical

to Canon (Baltimore: Johns Hopkins University Press, 1998) 84–95; M. Haran, "The Priestly Image of the Tabernacle," *HUCA* 36 (1965) 191–226; idem, "Shiloh and Jerusalem: The Origin of the Priestly Tradition in the Pentateuch," *JBL* 81 (1962) 14–24; idem, *Temples and Temple Service in Ancient Israel* (Oxford: Oxford University Press, 1978; repr. Winona Lake, Ind.: Eisenbrauns, 1985); R. E. Friedman, "The Tabernacle in the Temple," *BA* 43 (1980) 241–48; idem, *The Exile and Biblical Narrative* (HSM 22; Decatur, Ga.: Scholars Press, 1981); idem, "Tabernacle," *ABD* 6.292–300; M. Homan, *To Your Tents, O Israel! The Terminology, Function, Form, and Symbolism of Tents in the Hebrew Bible and the Ancient Near East* (Leiden: Brill, 2002); see also Y. Aharoni, "The Solomonic Temple, the Tabernacle, and the Arad Sanctuary," in *Orient and Occident* (Cyrus Gordon Festschrift; AOAT 1; ed. H. A. Hoffman Jr.; Neukirchen-Vluyn: Neukirchener Verlag, 1973).

4. Jeffrey H. Tigay (ed.), *Empirical Models for Biblical Criticism* (Philadelphia: University of Pennsylvania Press, 1985); cf. R. E. Friedman, "Some Recent Non-arguments Concerning the Documentary Hypothesis," in *Texts, Temples, and Traditions: A Tribute to Menahem Haran* (ed. Michael Fox et al.; Winona Lake, Ind.: Eisenbrauns, 1996) 87–101.

5. R. Moulton, *The Literary Study of the Bible* (London: Isbister, 1895); E. Auerbach, *Mimesis* (Princeton: Princeton University Press, 1953); N. Frye, *The Great Code* (New

scholars have made literary judgments without the sensitivities of the scholars who have spent years in training and study of other literatures and especially of comparative literature. For example, in six different studies, biblical scholars argued that the flood story was a unity marked by a chiastic structure and therefore could not be a composite of J and P. But, in every one of those studies, the chiasms were incorrectly identified, and sometimes the corresponding elements of the chiasms were both to be found within a single source, J or P, and so they presented no challenge to source analysis.[6] But as biblical scholars (who have been exceptionally open to contributions by nonspecialists) have become attracted to artistry analysis, we have begun to see better and better studies, which require the skills of both the literary critic and the traditional biblical scholar.

Such a merger, which is a relatively new development in the study of biblical prose, is better established in studies of poetry, which have been concerned for a long time with both artistry and literary history. A surge of works of poetic analysis in recent decades has served to remind us that we are still mystified by biblical poetry.[7] That there is still argument at such a basic level

---

York: Harcourt Brace Jovanovich, 1981); F. Kermode, *The Genesis of Secrecy* (Cambridge: Harvard University Press, 1979); R. Alter, "Sacred History and Prose Fiction," in *The Creation of Sacred Literature* (ed. R. E. Friedman; Near Eastern Studies 22; Berkeley: University of California Press, 1981) 7–24; idem, *The Art of Biblical Narrative* (New York: Basic, 1981); idem, *The Art of Biblical Poetry* (New York: Basic, 1985); Schneidau, *Sacred Discontent* (Berkeley: University of California Press, 1976); L. Brisman, *The Voice of Jacob* (Bloomington: Indiana University Press, 1990); D. Jacobson, *The Story of the Stories* (New York: Harper & Row, 1982).

6. I. M. Kikkawada and A. Quinn, *Before Abraham Was: The Unity of Genesis 1–11* (Nashville: Abingdon, 1985). I criticized this work on these grounds in "Some Recent Non-arguments Concerning the Documentary Hypothesis." J. A. Emerton criticized the other five on these grounds in "An Examination of Some Attempts to Defend the Unity of the Flood Narrative in Genesis"; the article appears in two parts: *VT* 37 (1987) 401–20; and *VT* 38 (1988) 1–21.

7. These include S. Geller, *Parallelism in Early Biblical Poetry* (HSM 20; Atlanta: Scholars Press, 1979); M. O'Connor, *Hebrew Verse Structure* (Winona Lake, Ind.: Eisenbrauns, 1980); J. Kugel, *The Idea of Biblical Poetry* (New Haven: Yale University Press, 1981); A. Berlin, *Poetics and Interpretation of Biblical Narrative* (Bible and Literature 9; Sheffield: Almond, 1983); *The Dynamics of Biblical Parallelism* (Bloomington: Indiana University Press, 1985); and numerous contributions by David Noel Freedman and Frank Moore Cross, including a new edition of their 1950 joint dissertation, *Studies in Ancient Yahwistic Poetry* (Grand Rapids, Mich.: Eerdmans, 1997), and Freedman's Prolegomenon to the new edition of G. B. Gray, *The Forms of Hebrew Poetry*, originally published in 1915 (New York: Ktav, 1972); as well as *Divine Commitment and Human Obligation: Selected Writings of David Noel Freedman*, volume 2: *Poetry and Orthography* (ed. John R. Huddlestun; Grand Rapids, Mich.: Eerdmans, 1997).

over the relationship of the parts of poetic parallel is extraordinary. The problem may be that scholarship still rarely breaks free from sequential reading of poetic texts. Whether scholars classify parallel lines of a bicolon as synonymous or antonymous, or describe them as "A and what's more B," or as patterns of intensification, they are still operating within a linear conception that is more suitable for biblical prose than for poetry. Like the rabbinic interpretations that sought to make subtle distinctions between the two halves of each biblical hendiadys, this kind of analysis of parallel does not fully come to terms with the combined image that the component lines form before us.

Meanwhile, there has been much discounting of quantitative analyses, almost always depicting them as less sophisticated than they are, when in fact the two scholars who are most identified with reckoning poetic syllable counts—David Noel Freedman and Frank Moore Cross—are at the same time probably the two most sensitive readers of Hebrew poetry. Recent and impressive in this regard are David Noel Freedman's quantitative syllabic analyses of acrostic and related poetry.[8] His results should impress even those who have most steadfastly resisted this mode of analysis. The poems show a regular overall structure that still allows room for internal variation. This may lead to a recognition of the relationship between this poetry and music, for this form of variation plus subsequent compensation to maintain overall structural regularity seems best explained as owing to musical accompaniment, and to percussion in particular.

As a point of methodology but also a point of aesthetics, taste, and appreciation, there is a need for more creative and sensitive readings of biblical poetry. When the psalmist says, "If I forget you, Jerusalem, let my right arm forget," we must get over feeling bound to insert a noun telling us what the right arm is supposed to forget.[9] One must have a feeling for poetry before one can analyze it. This should be obvious. But in our field it has not been.

The increased interest in literary artistry has also prompted concern with identifying the relationship between literary and historical criticism. This was a natural development in a field that has been dominated by history for so long. Hopefully, the debates and searches for a balance between the two in our generation will result in a productive merger rather than in an either-or. The Hebrew Bible was composed, after all, prior to the birth of the terms

---

8. D. N. Freedman, "Acrostic Poems in the Hebrew Bible: Alphabetic and Otherwise," *CBQ* 48 (1986); idem, *Psalm 119: The Exaltation of Torah* (Biblical and Judaic Studies from the University of California, San Diego, 6; Winona Lake, Ind.: Eisenbrauns, 1999).

9. This is not to ignore recent scholarship arguing that the term *tiškaḥ* in this famous verse (Ps 137:5) may instead play on the root for "forget" in the first half of the verse. I am simply making the point that the people who do not understand it to mean "forget" in both occurrences sometimes feel the need to add an object of the verb, which seems to me to lack sensitivity to the nature of poetry.

"literature" and "history"; and, ideally, our studies should be as polyvalent in their purposes as the biblical authors were.

The following are, to my mind, the main errors of our time. In publishing this list, I am inviting my colleagues in the field to identify what they also see as the primary errors of method—including my own. (There, I'm asking for it.)

Not Appreciating the Force of Evidence

Continuity of Sources

When the Torah's sources are separated from one another, we can usually observe each source flowing with narrative continuity. When we separate the J and P versions of the flood story, for example, we find that each is a complete narrative. Practically the whole of P and practically the whole of JE flow with this impressive continuity. Within JE, each source (J and E) often (but not always) has this continuity as well. This is an important piece of evidence supporting the entire hypothesis. It is also our best evidence for deducing how each editor worked. Yet it is rarely appreciated as even being important; much less is it responded to. A colleague criticized my division of the flood story into two continuous texts, saying that "of course" I had just divided them as needed to prove my point.[10] He did not grasp the point that no scholar is good enough to split a three-chapter story into two separate stories, each complete, each consistent with regard to the name of God used, each consistent with regard to all other terms without a single exception—and then to make each consistent with other stories that are traced to the same source. The flood story that is attributed to P never calls the deity by the name YHWH. The story that is attributed to J never refers to the deity as *ʾĕlōhîm*. The flood story that is attributed to P has the same construction of the universe as the creation story that is attributed to P. The flood story that is attributed to P has terms that are characteristic of other stories that are attributed to P. One can read two complete, continuous, unbroken narratives within the flood story—while keeping all these other factors consistent. The colleague who criticized me deserves credit for at least having commented on the point. Hardly one other scholar has even mentioned this fact in any book or article known to me. Scholars simply do not appreciate the force of the argument.

Linguistic Evidence

Especially in the early years of our field, scholars based their arguments for identifying and dating texts on factors such as: in what period would an

10. John Van Seters, "Scholars Face Off over Age of Biblical Stories," *Bible Review* 10/4 (1994) 40–44, 54.

author hold a certain theology, in what king's reign would a particular story fit. Such arguments may be right or wrong, but, methodologically, they lack the firmness of more concrete evidence, such as an archaeological artifact. One could always question the scholar's presumptions about what a writer might feel or express in a given period. One would have thought, therefore, that linguistic evidence would be particularly welcome as a more reliable basis for dating a text. The Hebrew Bible's early sources, after all, are separated from its latest sources by more centuries than the number of centuries that separate Shakespeare's English from mine. And in recent decades enormous strides have been made in identifying the stages of Biblical Hebrew's development, from classical preexilic Hebrew to late postexilic Hebrew. And there is outside corroboration: epigraphic discoveries coincide with classical Biblical Hebrew, while Qumran texts coincide with features of late Biblical Hebrew. One would think that there would be great excitement in the field over such research. But what has been the reaction in the field? Everyone whose model is not confirmed by this information simply ignores it. To date, no one has challenged it. Few have even mentioned it. If you bring up linguistic evidence in a conference session, they simply do not hear it. If you ask them why they do not respond to it, they do not answer the question—or even acknowledge that it was asked. Doing biblical scholarship without respect for Hebrew is like doing medicine without biology.[11]

Cumulative Argument

There is still insufficient appreciation of the cumulative argument. Making a cumulative argument does not mean piling on as much evidence as one can. It means showing how several discrete types of evidence all point to a common conclusion. A respectable scholar reviewing my *The Hidden Book in*

---

11. Avi Hurvitz, "The Relevance of Biblical Linguistics for the Historical Study of Ancient Israel," *Proceedings of the Twelfth World Congress of Jewish Studies* (Jerusalem: World Union of Jewish Studies, 1999) 21–33; "The Historical Quest for 'Ancient Israel' and the Linguistic Evidence of the Hebrew Bible: Some Methodological Observations," *VT* 47 (1997) 301–15; "Continuity and Innovation in Biblical Hebrew: The Case of 'Semantic Change' in Post-Exilic Writings," *AbrNSup* 4 (1995) 1–10; *A Linguistic Study of the Relationship between the Priestly Source and the Book of Ezekiel* (CahRB; Paris: Gabalda, 1982); "The Evidence of Language in Dating the Priestly Code," *RB* 81 (1974) 24–56; R. M. Polzin, *Late Biblical Hebrew: Toward an Historical Typology of Biblical Hebrew Prose* (HSM; Decatur, Ga.: Scholars Press, 1976); G. Rendsburg, "Late Biblical Hebrew and the Date of P," *JANES* 12 (1980) 65–80; Z. Zevit, "Converging Lines of Evidence Bearing on the Date of P," *ZAW* 94 (1982) 502–9 ; R. E. Friedman, "Solomon and the Great Histories," in *Jerusalem in Bible and Archaeology: The First Temple Period* (ed. Ann Killebrew and Andrew Vaughn; Atlanta: Society of Biblical Literature, 2003) 171–80; *The Hidden Book in the Bible* (San Francisco: HarperCollins, 1998) 362.

the Bible said, "Friedman himself must admit that the argument is a cumulative one."[12] I did not *admit* that it was a cumulative argument. I *declared* that it was a cumulative argument. The convergence of multiple lines of the evidence was itself an argument for the theory. Our colleagues in the physical sciences appreciate this sort of phenomenon in the acquisition and presentation of evidence. It still eludes most of our colleagues in fields of the humanities in which rigor is not expected.

Mistaking Skill at Critique for Skill at Contribution

It is not that difficult to find flaws in the models of the great synthesists. Researchers who are not as great as Freud are still able to identify individual errors within Freud's big picture. Likewise in our field, scholars have been able to harvest the errors in the great model-makers: Wellhausen, Albright. Especially great intuitive scholars make leaps that enable them to make important advances but that leave errors on the trail, which later scholars have the task of identifying and evaluating relative to the advance. But the error-spotters have sometimes therefore been mistaken by others (and themselves) for major model-makers in their own right. Building a satisfactory alternative to the model whose flaws one has seen, however, is something different. Thus, some scholars performed a very helpful service early in their careers by showing weaknesses in Wellhausen and Albright. But the very same scholars then put forth models that were not in a class with the models that they had challenged.

Not Distinguishing between Writers and Their Sources

What was missing in the early days of our field was a connection from the sources back to the whole. What did JEP and D have to do with The Bible? And when the whole *was* treated, especially in studies of literary artistry, the source texts were generally ignored. Now we are getting studies of the whole, and we are getting redaction criticism, addressing the process by which the parts came together. Yet we still find scholars blatantly ignoring the distinction between biblical tradents and their sources. In the case of the Chronicler's work, we still find the extraordinarily common assumption in our field

---

12. Lawrence Schiffman, *The Forward* (November 27, 1998), p. 1. John Barton, reviewing the same work, better understood the nature of cumulative argument, pointing out that the way to deal with such an argument is by rigorous testing of each individual part; *JJS* 52 (2001). I emphasized the role of the cumulative argument in *The Hidden Book in the Bible*, 326ff., 351–52, 361–62.

that if it's in Chronicles it's late.[13] Likewise, there are those who attribute practically the whole of the Deuteronomistic history to the Deuteronomistic historian, as if he had written it all himself—when, in fact, it is some 80 to 90 percent sources that he incorporated. And, especially in literary studies of the Pentateuch, we find scholars who attribute the whole of the Torah to the redactor, as if he were its author and not its editor. If we lived in a world of Old Testament justice, then those who publish these things would have to have their own writing credited to *their* editors. That is a pretty unpleasant thought, especially when one considers that the biblical editors had what contemporary editors can only dream of: all of their authors were dead.

Anachronistic Judgments

Reading one's current values into antiquity is an easy slip to make, and we must always be on our self-critical guard against it. I may never live down my mistake of referring to the prophet Amos as a "cowboy" in *Who Wrote the Bible?* I misunderstood that this term refers specifically to those who herd cattle while riding a horse, and it has no place in ancient Israel. D. Winton Thomas made the mistake of picturing his own world in place of the prophet Zechariah's in his commentary on Zech 8:5. The prophet pictures a happy time when "the streets of the city will be filled with boys and girls, playing in its streets." Thomas expresses his concern that we may be shocked at the idea of children playing out in the street. He seems to have in mind a world in which automobiles speed through city streets, rather than an ancient Israelite town square. For another example, see Michael Homan's essay in this book. He notes that even a fine scholar such as Jack Sasson and a skilled archaeologist such as Lawrence Stager judge beer to be socially inferior to wine in ancient Israel, basing this appraisal on their perceptions of the current relative social status of the two drinks. And then there is the fact that Bible movies continue to picture medieval Bedouin headdress on biblical characters. Anachronism is an easy mistake to make because, despite the archaeological revolution, we still know so little of life in ancient Israel and its closest neighbors.

---

13. Victor (Avigdor) Hurowitz, "The Form and Fate of the Tabernacle: Reflections on a Recent Proposal," *JQR* 86 (1995) 127–51. The article is a challenge to my work on the Tabernacle. Hurowitz simply discounts evidence from Chronicles, noting that it is a later text than Kings, claiming that the Chronicler equates the Tabernacle and the Temple, with no examination of the time of its sources or even recognition that it contains sources, and a misunderstanding of its relationship with Kings. He declares: "any independent statement of the Chronicler must be assumed suspect unless proven otherwise." This and other methodological errors in Hurowitz's analysis have been criticized in Homan, *To Your Tents, O Israel!*

Taking Prophets' Criticisms as Factual

In recent decades we have become ever more cautious and critical in our judgments of the biblical books of historical narrative. A comparable sort of historical skepticism has not always been applied to the books of the prophets. In standard introductions to the Hebrew Bible, in volumes on the history of Israel, and in commentaries on the prophets, one frequently finds that scholars take the prophet's word for it whenever the prophet speaks of the society of his day. If the prophet criticizes his people for pagan practices, the scholar writes that there was a problem of widespread pagan practices at that time. If the prophet criticizes people's unfairness to the poor, the scholar decries the economic inequity of the time. If the prophet criticizes corruption or perverse behavior, the scholar concludes that corruption and perversity were rampant. Worst of all, if the prophet criticizes the people's sacrifices, the scholar concludes that the prophet was against sacrifice. It is a commonplace to assume that in Jeremiah's time the people believed that the Temple and/or Jerusalem was inviolable. An analogy would be to judge the character of American society of the twentieth century on the basis of critical sermons by individual ministers or rabbis. To round out the analogy, we should make it only the sermons that a particular religious community chose to preserve.

Methodologically, we must feel bound instead to treat the prophetic writings as evidence. What they show is an individual's perspective of his people's condition. The prophets are insightful, gifted witnesses, and we must be grateful to have their texts; but we cannot accept their judgments uncritically. They themselves reveal openly that there were contemporary prophets who disagreed with them. They have conflicting perspectives among themselves (for example, Jeremiah's and Ezekiel's different views of priesthood and sacred texts). And both the prophets and the Deuteronomic law warn of the difficulty of distinguishing between true and false prophecy. Furthermore, it is a prophet's job to point out to his people their shortcomings, not to spend his days praising what they have already done right. The evidence from the prophets, therefore, by its very nature focuses disproportionately on the negative. To base one's picture of the biblical world uncautiously on their texts is necessarily to err by expanding this negative judgment out of its proper proportion as a description of their society's full character.

Assuming the Existence of "Schools"
without Substantial Evidence

Scholars in our field continue to write about schools (and movements and circles): the J school, the E school, the Wisdom school, the Priestly school, the Scribal school, and the Deuteronomistic school. Some or all of these groups may have existed. Some or all may not. What is wrong with so many scholarly studies of them is that (1) they *presume* the existence of these schools, never so much as attempting to prove it; and (2) they do not explain what a school is. What was the nature of the society? Where and when and how did they meet? What gave them their common identity? In my contribution to another Festschrift for David Noel Freedman, I wrote about the so-called Deuteronomistic school, that

> every now and then a notion comes to be firmly fixed in the discourse of our field and even comes to be generally accepted without really having been proven or even systematically assembled. One of these is the matter of the Deuteronomistic school. It is a commonplace of scholarship on the Hebrew Bible to speak of this school and to identify the work of its members on numerous books of biblical narrative and prophecy. We do not know exactly who they were, what the nature of their association was, or why they apparently were so rigidly bound to using a fixed group of terms and phrases. Still, they are assumed to have existed, maintaining their particular identity and looking after their particular interests through one generation after another for centuries. They are claimed to have produced major biblical works—including the Deuteronomistic history, the longest work in the Bible—and they are claimed to have acquired copies of numerous other works, from JE to Amos to portions of Jeremiah, and to have added words, phrases, and lines to them so as to make their own ideas appear to have been part of these works.
>
> Thus the literature of the field is filled with expressions such as the "Deuteronomistic school," the "Deuteronomistic circle of tradition," the "Deuteronomistic party," the "Deuteronomistic movement," "Deuteronomistic stylistic forms," "Deuteronomistically colored passages," and "Deuteronomistically influenced traditionists." The vagueness of these terms, in the absence of clear referents in history, and in the absence of clear conceptions of the literary processes involved, is a major weakness in the entire enterprise and a serious threat to our progress in this area. As long as we biblical scholars continue to use these non-specific, non-descriptive terms and categories, it is no wonder that literary scholars, especially comparatists, look upon us as unsophisticated.[14]

What I wrote about the "Deuteronomistic school" there might be said about other hypothetical schools as well. When we use the terms without real proof or at least strong indicators of their existence and character, we veil the literary process and the social process as well.

---

14. R. E. Friedman, "The Deuteronomistic School," in *Fortunate the Eyes That See: Esaays in Honor of David Noel Freedman in Celebration of His Seventieth Birthday* (ed. Astrid Beck et al.; Grand Rapids, Mich.: Eerdmans, 1995) 70–71.

Assuming the Existence of Oral Forerunners of Written Works

One of the most nebulous areas of discussion in biblical scholarship has always been the oral pre-stage of the written text. This vagueness is certainly understandable, a result of the inherent difficulty in getting at oral developments, short of having a time machine. The evidence is simply difficult to establish. Indeed, some scholars have emphasized the oral stage of biblical composition with little evidence that there *was* an oral stage or without getting at the degree to which any given written text was related to this hypothetical oral stage. When we read the words of a biblical text, are they the writer's own words or not? Is the wordplay his own or not? Is the ending of the story the writer's own or not? And so on. The fact is that there is some, but little, evidence that J or E was based partly on something oral. And there is almost no chance that Dtr or P was originally oral. We can see the written sources on which the latter were based. And we can observe and describe the *literary* process of their composition. We can say the same of the Chronicler's work and of much of the material of the sources of the Deuteronomistic history.

Reinventing the Wheel

When we say that the study of literary artistry is a new development in the field, this statement is, to some extent, misleading. Literary (in the sense of artistic) observation of the biblical text has always gone on, from medieval to modern scholarship—only not as independently from other biblical concerns as it does now. Scholars did not put a banner with the word "literary" over their research. Rather, literary criticism was simply an integral part of the process. It dealt with many of the same sorts of observations as did literary criticism of other works but not in the same format or with the explicit theoretical structure of general literary criticism. What we are witnessing today is not really the arrival of something new but the disengagement of the study of literary artistry from other forms of biblical analysis. It must be said: the literary critics who have asserted that literary criticism has not been used in the field have simply been ignorant of the field.

What the field has seen is the beginning of a more sensitive, self-conscious, and defined focus on artistry. So far, it has been largely descriptive, identifying the components that make up the work. It has involved close reading of text, observation of the techniques of allusion and wordplay, narrative strategy, and a substantial amount of structural study. There has been minimal focus on the authors comparable to the amount found in criticism of the literature of other cultures and periods, and there has been minimal focus on editorial artistry. The editors are used more as an artificial construct, a practice that has the effect of avoiding issues of authorship and editing.

Thus far we have had minimal comparative study of technique: for example, of the way that the P source tells the story of the flood, the Abrahamic covenant, the exodus and Red Sea events, and so on—as opposed to the ways that the J or E sources tell the same stories; or a coming to terms with such possibilities as that the author of P had read J and E and composed P as a complement or an alternative to them; or a recognition, against nineteenth-century theological prejudices, that P involves some artful writing.

The overall point is that all of these areas—form criticism, source criticism, redaction criticism, and artistry criticism—are components of one process, the literary process. And we must perform all of them to know and interpret that process. If there are scholars who choose to work in only one of them, that is their personal choice. But the methodological agenda of our *field* must be to deal with all of them in synthesis.

The Need for Cooperation

At the beginning of this essay, I criticized colleagues who write outside of their areas of expertise. I want to add now that I do not mean by this that they should not write about these things at all. The methodological point is rather that, in an age of ever-narrowing specialization, what we need is to cooperate. When we find that our research leads us into areas beyond our professional reach, we need to consult. It is ironic and unfortunate that, in an age when we need to be doing interdisciplinary sharing and cooperation, we have biblical scholars arguing about inscriptions when they are not trained in epigraphy, and arguing about the dates of texts when they are insufficiently knowledgeable in Hebrew linguistics. And we find biblical archaeologists arguing about the composition of biblical texts when they are not trained or even well read in biblical scholarship and are clueless about the complexity of biblical sources and editing.

It was one thing when we were criticizing Harold Bloom, Karen Armstrong, and Dr. Laura. They did not *look* like someone who should know anything about the Bible. So whoever read them and trusted in them got what they deserved. But it is another thing when biblical scholars fool with the tools of archaeology and when archaeologists of the land of Israel fool with the Bible, because there is a presumption that they know what they are talking about. This presumption comes first from the fact that the two fields are related, and second from the fact that there were early greats in our field who really did both: giants such as Albright and G. E. Wright. But the explosion of knowledge—and the supernova of publication of books and articles—has driven us all more and more to specialization: which is to say, to limitation.

We can accept the new reality of our field that it is no longer possible to read everything on a subject, but we can still understand that everyone must know the founding works that brought us where we are. No one should be writing about the Hebrew Bible's sources without knowing Wellhausen, Driver, and Noth. One cannot read everything, so one must use wisdom and common sense in choosing what one reads—and in recognizing what one cannot afford *not* to read. And no one should be doing *anything* in our field without knowing the development of Hebrew.

Finally, we should take notice of what has been the broadest development, crossing all of these areas, in this period—namely, the self-conscious concern with method. There has been serious questioning of the assumptions and approaches through which we collect evidence and evaluate it and how we formulate and test hypotheses. There have been a number of conferences and volumes addressing methodological questions, including four of our San Diego conferences and the resulting volumes,[15] and the present volume as well. But, really, a methodological consciousness appears to me to be interspersed through a variety of works in the field, to the extent that current works that lack this sense of method seem incomplete. It might well become the most gratifying aspect of our generation's contribution to the literary study of the Bible if we come to be known as an age of method. We finally have enough data and enough history of scholarship behind us to have a sense of what the most productive questions are, and we have the tools to answer them.

---

15. R. E. Friedman (ed.), *Creation of Sacred Literature* (Near Eastern Studies 22; Berkeley: University of California Press, 1981); idem, *The Poet and the Historian: Essays in Literary and Historical Biblical Criticism* (HSS 26; Atlanta: Scholars Press, 1983); R. E. Friedman and H. G. M. Williamson (eds.), *The Future of Biblical Studies: The Hebrew Scriptures* (Semeia Studies; Atlanta: Scholars Press, 1987); W. H. Propp, B. Halpern, and D. N. Freedman (eds.), *The Hebrew Bible and Its Interpreters* (Biblical and Judaic Studies from the University of California, San Diego 1; Winona Lake, Ind.: Eisenbrauns, 1990).

Chapter 2

Symbolic Wounds:
Applying Anthropology to the Bible

WILLIAM H. C. PROPP

Like our father, Jacob, David Noel Freedman walks with a slight limp acquired in athletic contest. I do not know what role this injury played in turning Noel decisively toward the life of the intellect, or whether in his mind it marked a transition from juvenility to adulthood (the age of the incident was twelve or thirteen). But it is a convenient point from which to launch an investigation of various injuries, real and symbolic, that mark turning points in the lives of biblical characters.

Initiation Rites

Throughout the world, major life changes are celebrated and effected by rites of passage.[1] The subject leaves his/her prior society, undergoes a transformation, then rejoins that society with a changed status and new peer set. The middle, "liminal" stage often involves a symbolic death and resurrection and some sort of "initiatory mutilation": a haircut, scarification, loss of a tooth or a digit, circumcision, subincision, etc. Initiation is particularly prominent in stone age and hunter-gatherer societies and presumably belongs to our common human heritage. We will probably never move beyond the fraternity hazing, military bootcamp, Ph.D. defense, and so forth.[2]

---

1. The classic study is Arnold van Gennep, *Les rites de passage* (Paris: Emile Nourry, 1909). More recently, see Mircea Eliade, *Rites and Symbols of Initiation* (New York: Harper & Row, 1958); Victor Turner, *The Forest of Symbols* (Ithaca: Cornell University Press, 1967) 93–111; and J. S. La Fontaine, *Initiation* (Manchester: Manchester University Press, 1985).

2. For a fascinating study of rites of initiation among ultraorthodox Jews, superficially light years apart from New Guinea villagers, see Yoram Bilu, "Circumcision, the

It is no coincidence that these last examples of "Western" initiation were, until recently, performed by older *men* upon younger *men*. Rituals of male initiation, particularly those associated with puberty, are strikingly similar across cultures. With his innate capacity for violence, with his innate need to establish a place in the social hierarchy, with his innate urge to reproduce, with his innate need to define himself against the women who bore and raised him—the volatile male evidently needs some external ritual control, lest he turn on society and on himself. The drama of death and rebirth unmistakably articulates Man's perennial dread, from the Stone Age to the Clone Age, that he may ultimately prove superfluous to the survival of the species.

Concerning the "initiatory mutilation" per se, initiators, initiates, and scholarly analysts proffer many explanations: it enhances beauty, strength, and/or fertility; it instills, through fear, a proper respect for elders and societal norms; it is a sign of adulthood and/or group membership, symbolizing and creating solidarity horizontally with one's peers and vertically with past and future generations; it betokens eligibility for marriage; it is the symbolic death of the initiate's former social status and his bloody rebirth to a new status; it is a symbolic severing of the umbilical cord, draining the boy's "female blood"; it symbolizes a separation between childhood and adulthood, or between male and female; it is a preemptive sacrifice to inevitable Misfortune, lest more serious injuries ensue; it is an ordeal to prove self-control and/or impress the opposite sex; the cutting emulates the gods' Creation; the pain both enhances and is palliated by the initiate's altered state; the pain and mutilation act together as a mnemonic aid for information imparted during initiation, and so forth. Initiatory circumcision and subincision have even been understood as attempts to endow men with female properties.[3] The most convincing explanation I know, however, is that surrendering part of oneself is a behavior deeply rooted in evolution. Just as an animal will shed a limb to escape a predator's grasp, so we sacrifice a nonessential body member to a superior Power, call it God or Society.[4]

It seems that, at the deepest level, "initiatory mutilation" has no real meaning at all. The act is its own justification: a good ritual, like a good poem, sustains multiple interpretations. But it must be powerful: beautiful, orgiastic, loud, terrifying, or painful.

First Haircut, and the Torah: Ritual and Male Identity in the Ultraorthodox Community of Israel," in *Imagined Masculinities: Male Identity and Culture in the Modern Middle East* (ed. M. Ghoussoub and E. Sinclair Weiss; London: Saqi, 2000) 33–64.

3. Bruno Bettelheim, *Symbolic Wounds* (London: Thames & Hudson, 1955), who provided the inspiration for my title.

4. Walter Burkert, *Creation of the Sacred* (Cambridge: Harvard University Press, 1996) 34–35.

The "Branding" Motif

Even in cultures that do not practice adolescent initiation, popular narratives may follow a pattern reminiscent of rites of passage. In 1946, folklorist Vladimir I. Propp noted the similarity between heroic tales and initiation, suggesting that the former evolved out of the latter.[5] A "Proppian" tale features a male protagonist, an initial problem, a journey, an adversary, a donor, a battle, and a return. For our purposes, it is important to add that Propp identified in many fairy tales a motif of "branding." This is a mark or wound acquired before or during the contest with the villain. Whether real or symbolic, this injury often possesses a protective power.[6]

Unlike Vladimir Propp, I do not assume that heroic tales necessarily arose out of actual initiatory rites. Doubtless, humans (chiefly men?) are conditioned by nature and nurture to respond to this sequence of acts, whether they actually undergo it or are merely told about it.[7] In the following pages, I shall demonstrate that Israelite literature, both narrative and legal, frequently features the "brand" or "initiatory mutilation."[8] Not all cases feature actual injuries, admittedly. Sometimes an animal is slain instead; sometimes one's "second skin," that is, one's clothing, is harmed; sometimes one's hair is painlessly shorn. These are "symbolic wounds" in two senses: they metaphorically represent injuries, which in turn symbolize a changed social status.[9]

---

5. For an English translation, see V. I. Propp, *Theory and History of Folklore* (Theory and History of Literature 5; Minneapolis: University of Minnesota Press, 1984) 116–23; see also Eliade, *Rites and Symbols*, 124–28. Propp's thesis runs parallel to the "Myth and Ritual School" of Near Eastern and biblical studies; see John W. Rogerson, *Myth in Old Testament Interpretation* (BZAW 134; Berlin: de Gruyter, 1974) 66–84. Myth and Ritual drew inspiration from James Frazer's *Golden Bough* and from William Robertson Smith, who wrote, "in almost every case the myth was derived from the ritual, and not the ritual from the myth; for the ritual was fixed and the myth was variable, the ritual was obligatory and faith in the myth was at the discretion of the worshipper" (*Lectures on the Religion of the Semites* [3rd ed.; New York: Macmillan, 1927] 18).

6. See V. I. Propp, *The Morphology of the Folktale* (2nd ed.; Russian original, 1928; Austin: University of Texas Press, 1968).

7. Burkert (*Creation of the Sacred*, 63–67) traces the origin of the quest story to the primal search for food—and, I would add, a mate.

8. Although full discussion would take us too far afield, the w/tomb symbolism of the rite of passage is evident in many biblical passages that lack the symbolic injury theme (e.g., Hos 6:1–2; Jonah 2; Ps 9:14; 16:10; 23:4 [?]; 30; 71:20).

9. Not all mutilations are positive, naturally. Some create social stigma (Lev 21:17–23; Deut 23:2), just as imperfect animals may not be sacrificed (Lev 22:20; Deut 15:21; 17:1; Mal 1:14). See further Saul Olyan, *Rites and Rank* (Princeton: Princeton University Press, 2000) 103–14.

Initiatory Wounds in the Hebrew Bible

a. The first human, originally both childlike and beastlike, becomes a heterosexual, adult male after Yahweh opens a wound in his side and extracts Eve (Gen 2:21–24).

b. When Cain, the fratricide, is condemned to nomadism, having previously tilled the soil, Yahweh gives him a sign that will protect him from Abel's would-be avengers (Gen 4:14–15). Whether this is a bodily sign is unclear.[10]

c. Although generally regarded as Abraham's trial, from Isaac's perspective the Akedah (Genesis 22) recalls a rite of passage. The passive child is separated from his mother, taken by his father on a lonely quest, nearly killed, and then brought home.[11] But there is a twist: the wound is not pars pro toto (as in circumcision) but vicarious (that is, the ram is slain).

d. The biography of Jacob (essentially, Gen 25:19–34; 27–33; 35) bears a limited similarity to the Proppian model.[12] Threatened by his brother Esau, Jacob must flee his home, ultimately spending twenty years abroad. The end and climax of his exile is a nocturnal wrestling bout with a divine being (Gen 32:25–32), recapitulating his in utero tussling with Esau (Gen 25:22).[13] It ends in a stalemate, with Jacob injured and the angel unable to escape. Jacob emerges from the Jabbok an altered character. No longer a schemer, no longer able to dislodge boulders single-handedly, no longer a procreator, the renamed "Israel" is a handicapped senior citizen, less an actor and more acted upon.

e. When the men of Shechem propose to intermarry with Jacob's people, Simeon and Levi require the Shechemites to undergo circumcision to signify that the two peoples have become a single endogamous kinship group (Gen 34:14–17).[14]

f. A somewhat more subtle case is Joseph, exiled to Egypt by his brothers. Instead of killing him and "hiding his blood," they sell him into slavery, take his coat, and dip it in goat blood (Gen 37:26–35). This creates a symbolic injury that misleads their father, Jacob, as Joseph descends in social status.

10. Cf. Ezek 9:4 and Rev 7:3 for protective signs on the forehead.

11. Nancy Jay (*Throughout Your Generations Forever* [Chicago: University of Chicago Press, 1992] 102) describes the Akedah as a "spiritual 'birth' accomplished without female assistance," ensuing in the promise of numberless descendants.

12. See Pamela J. Milne, *Vladimir Propp and the Study of Structure in Hebrew Biblical Narrative* (Bible and Literature Series 13; Sheffield: Almond, 1988) 125–44.

13. Compare Hos 12:4–5. Jacob's adversary appears to be a star god come to earth, comparable to Helel of Isa 14:12. At any rate, he cannot abide beyond the dawn.

14. That such may have been circumcision's original significance among the Semites is often inferred from the dual meanings of Arabic *ḥatana*: 'become related by marriage' and 'circumcise' (e.g., Julius Wellhausen, *Reste arabischen Heidentums* [2nd ed.; Berlin: de Gruyter, 1927] 175).

g. Prior to his rehabilitation by Pharaoh, Joseph shaves his hair and changes his clothes (Gen 41:14).[15]

h. Moses is apparently threatened by Yahweh on the way back to Egypt (Exod 4:24–26). Although much is unclear, it seems that Moses is saved by Zipporah's application of circumcision blood to his genitals.[16] This symbolic injury marks the end of Moses' career as a brawler and procreator (Exod 2:11–22) and the start of his career as a liberator and Lawgiver.[17]

i. As they change status from slave to free, the people of Israel place upon their houses a symbolic wound ensuring Yahweh's protection during the traumatic Passover night (Exod 12:7, 13, 22–23). Comparative ethnography suggests that the ritual originally repelled demons, tricking them into believing a death had already occurred.[18] The mark is only temporary, but it is renewed annually in the original form of the paschal rite.[19]

j. According to Exod 21:6, a Hebrew slave who chooses to remain a lifelong bondsman must have his ear pierced (also Deut 15:17). This injury marks him as a perpetual slave.

k. In Exod 24:5–8, Moses applies sacrificial blood to the people as they enter into covenant with God. This symbolic wound is the mirror image of the paschal blood. Again an animal dies, and Israel is bloodied. But this time they pass from liberty into servitude to Yahweh.[20]

l. A more explicit initiation is the inauguration of the High Priest (Exodus 29; Leviticus 8). Sacrificial blood is applied to his right ear, thumb, and big toe (Exod 29:20; Lev 8:23–24). As in Exodus 24, the rest of the blood is spattered against the altar. By now the symbolism should be clear. The ear is symbolically injured, like that of the perpetual slave (Exod 21:6; Deut 15:17); the digits are symbolically severed, like those of Adoni Bezek's captives (Judg 1:6–7).[21] By symbolically forfeiting nonessential body parts, the Levite is transformed into a priest, Yahweh's bondsman and the paragon of purity.

---

15. On hair-cutting in the context of rites of passage and the Bible, see Saul Olyan, "What Do Shaving Rites Accomplish and What Do They Signal in Biblical Ritual Contexts?" *JBL* 117 (1998) 611–22.

16. For this and alternative readings, see my "That Bloody Bridegroom," *VT* 43 (1993) 495–518.

17. See my *Exodus 1–18* (AB 2; New York: Doubleday, 1999) 33, 233, 240.

18. Ibid., 434–39.

19. Ibid., 445–52.

20. Although he does not invoke the symbolic wound per se, Ronald S. Hendel ("Sacrifice as a Cultural System: The Ritual Symbolism of Exodus 24,3–8," *ZAW* 101 [1989] 366–90) compares Exod 24:3–8 to rites of passage and the blood spattering to signs such as circumcision and the paschal blood.

21. Adoni Bezek's mutilation of his captives could also be regarded as betokening a changed social status. The Philistines (Judg 16:21), Nahash the Ammonite (1 Sam 11:2)

m. When Moses descends from Mount Sinai in his new capacity as Law-giver, his skin is in some way transformed. According to the majority view, he shines with a divine light (Exod 34:29–35). By another interpretation, however, he is disfigured, his skin unnaturally toughened, an unsightly sign of his intimacy with Yahweh and a protection against harm.[22]

n. An antitype to the pure priest is the defiled "leper" (i.e., one afflicted with a skin disease). When he is fully purified, sacrificial blood is placed on his right ear, thumb, and big toe. But in this case, oil is then applied to these areas as well as the head (Lev 14:14–17). Hair-shaving is also required (Lev 13:33; 14:8–9).

o. Another antitype to the priest is the mourner, since the presence of death defiles, and priests are ordinarily forbidden to touch corpses or mourn (Lev 21:1–5). To betoken one's temporary status as mourner, one tears one's garment (Gen 37:29, 34; 44:13; 2 Sam 1:2, etc.)—a symbolic wound—and covers oneself with dirt and/or ashes (Isa 58:5; Jer 6:26; 25:34; Ezek 27:30; Lam 3:16; Esth 4:1, 3; Dan 9:3), which frequently represent death in rites of passage.[23] A mourner might also crop his/her hair or inflict minor self-injury (Lev 21:5; Deut 14:1; Isa 15:2; 22:12; Jer 16:6; 41:5; 47:5; 48:37; Amos 8:10; Job 1:20).

p. Similarly, Tamar rips her garment and covers herself with ashes to in-dicate her new status as nonvirgin (2 Sam 13:19).

q. When the Levites are set apart for divine service, they must shave their entire bodies and wash their garments (Num 8:6–7).

r. The Nazirite is deconsecrated by cutting his holy hair, which is burned upon the altar (Num 6:18). In Samson's case, this entails loss of supernatural strength (Judges 16).

s. A captive woman entering into concubinage must shave her head, pare her nails, change her garments, and mourn for a month (Deut 21:12–13).

---

and Nebuchadnezzar (2 Kgs 25:7) put out the eyes, while David collects Philistine foreskins (1 Sam 18:25–27). More moderate, Nahash's son Hanun merely shaves his captives and modifies their clothing (2 Sam 10:4). The punitive mutilation of criminals similarly signi-fies a new social classification (Exod 21:24–25 and parallels; Deut 25:12).

22. W. H. C. Propp, "The Skin of Moses' Face: Transfigured or Disfigured?" *CBQ* 49 (1987) 375–86.

23. V. Turner (*The Forest of Symbols,* 96) notes, "The metaphor of dissolution is often applied to neophytes; they are allowed to go filthy and identified with the earth, the gen-eralized matter into which every specific individual is rendered down." On p. 202 he notes the prominence of ashes as a symbol of death. Writing on masculine psychology and ini-tiation, Robert Bly entitles a chapter "The Road of Ashes, Descent, and Grief" (*Iron John* [Reading: Addison-Wesley, 1990] 56–91).

t. Of all the prophets, Isaiah provides the most detailed account of his initiation to prophecy. In a vision, an angel cauterizes his impure lips with a glowing coal, permitting him to transmit God's holy words (Isa 6:5–7).

u. I have so far referred only obliquely to the Bible's most obvious "initiatory mutilation": the rite of circumcision. One may infer from the Bible that, as in most other cultures, Israelite circumcision was not originally performed upon infants but was instead a rite of passage into adulthood. [24] Yet the Priestly Source mandates infant circumcision on the eighth day (Genesis 17). Among the reasons for this shift are P's polemic against clan religion, in which adolescent initiation may have played a role, [25] and a belief that the uncircumcised suffer in the Afterlife, much like the unbaptized in Christianity. [26] I would now add a third factor. As I have mentioned, rites of passage characteristically act out the initiate's death and rebirth. Born of woman, raised by and among women, the boy is rebirthed by men as a man. But once metaphor builds a bridge between properly distinct concepts, symbolism can flow in either direction. As rites of puberty mimic true birth, so the rites of birth may come to imitate rites of puberty—in this case, by incorporating the "initiatory mutilation." [27] A mark signifying the social separation from women in general now betokens the physical separation from a single woman—that is, the mother. [28]

v. Finally, many of the themes we have been studying converge in Joshua 5. Symbolically reborn in the Jordan, [29] the people circumcise themselves and celebrate the Passover. [30] Joshua encounters Yahweh's "commander," evidently the sort of bellicose angel that Jacob once beheld at Mahanaim (Gen 32:2–3) and battled in the Jabbok (Gen 32:25–32). The ceremonies at Gilgal are Israel's rite of reincorporation into Canaan, after their liminal centuries in Egypt and the wilderness.

---

24. See my "Origins of Infant Circumcision in Israel," *HAR* 11 (1987) 355–70.

25. Propp, *Exodus 1–18,* 237, with reference to Baruch Halpern, "Jerusalem and the Lineages in the Seventh Century B.C.E.: Kinship and the Rise of Individual Moral Liability," in *Law and Ideology in Monarchic Israel* (ed. B. Halpern and D. W. Hobson; JSOTSup 124; Sheffield: JSOT Press, 1991) 11–107.

26. On the degradation of the uncircumcised dead, see Ezek 28:10; 31:18; 32:19–32.

27. Thus, one could even view infant circumcision as a by-product of the war between the sexes, with women reclaiming for the home men's secret, pseudo–birth rite (note Zipporah circumcising her son in Exod 4:24–26).

28. I owe this formulation to Elizabeth Goldstein.

29. On water and (re)birth imagery, see my *Exodus 1–18,* 157–58, 562.

30. The connection between circumcision and the Passover was already adumbrated in Exod 12:48; see my *Exodus 1–18,* 452–54. Joshua's circumcision may also be foreshadowed in Deut 10:11, 16, "Rise, go on the journey before the people, so they may come and possess the land. . . . Circumcise your hearts' foreskins."

Applying Anthropology to the Bible

Anthropology has much to teach the Bible scholar. While we cannot interrogate the biblical authors or their fellow citizens of Israel, we can converse with modern peoples of similar lifestyles and comparable customs. The result is often a greater appreciation of the symbolic undercurrents of biblical literature.

There is also some danger, to be sure. We must avoid recklessly filling in lacunae in our knowledge with isolated data culled from ethnography. A more legitimate use of anthropology is to draw our attention to the atypical. From the vantage point of comparative ethnography, it is slightly peculiar that Israel and the other societies of the ancient Near East did not practice adolescent male initiation. We might predict, and indeed we find, that the immemorial ritual complex was sublimated, popping up in literary contexts precisely because initiation had lost its centrality in day-to-day life.

Chapter 3
Beer, Barley, and שֵׁכָר in the Hebrew Bible

MICHAEL M. HOMAN

Ninkasi, the Sumerian goddess of beer, was praised for her ability to warm the liver and sate the heart.[1] When one accounts for ancient Near Eastern conceptions of organ function, in which the liver controlled emotions and the heart cognition, it is fitting that I dedicate this paper concerning beer to my teacher and friend David Noel Freedman in celebration of his 80th birthday. David Noel Freedman is truly a beer god for the modern era because, more than anyone in his field, his charm has warmed countless hearts, and for generations to come his multitudinous publications and edited volumes will intoxicate thirsty minds beyond satiation.

Introduction to the Problem of the Identity of שֵׁכָר

"What is the difference between wine (יַיִן) and שֵׁכָר?" Rabbi Yose the Galilean was justifiably confused when he asked this important question in the second century C.E.[2] According to the Hebrew Bible, שֵׁכָר was a vital component in ancient Israelite religion. Four hins (≈16 liters) of שֵׁכָר were libated to Yahweh weekly (Num 28:7–10).[3] The Israelites drank שֵׁכָר along with wine at sacrificial meals (Deut 14:26), and both beverages were forbidden to

---

1. *Hymn to Ninkasi*, lines 51–52; 61–63; 75. See Miguel Civil, "A Hymn to the Beer Goddess and a Drinking Song," in *Studies Presented to A. Leo Oppenheim* (Chicago: University of Chicago Press, 1964) 67–89. Cf. *The Epic of Gilgamesh*, in which, after seven cups of beer, Enkidu's "soul became free and cheerful, his heart rejoiced, and his face glowed" (OB version, 2.3.19–21).

2. *Num. Rab.* 10:8, commenting on Num 6:3.

3. It is unclear where the libation of שֵׁכָר was to take place. According to Num 28:7, the שֵׁכָר was to be poured out בַּקֹּדֶשׁ, an unspecified area located somewhere in the Tabernacle. In addition to שֵׁכָר, wine was libated on the Tabernacle's altar (Num 15:5–10). Wine libations are also prescribed at the beginning of each month (Num 28:14), though the liquid libated is ambiguous in the Syriac and Vulgate, and it is absent in Ezek 46:6–7. See Morris Jastrow Jr., "Wine in the Pentateuchal Codes," *JAOS* 33 (1913) 180–92.

Nazirites (Num 6:3; Judg 13:4, 7, 14)[4] and to priests entering the Tabernacle (Lev 10:9).[5] Secular aspects of the Hebrew Bible further illustrate the significance of שֵׁכָר. Its overconsumption was condemned (Isa 5:11; 28:7; Prov 20:1; 31:4). However, the absence of שֵׁכָר signified a melancholy occasion (Isa 24:9), and it was prescribed to the forlorn to temporarily erase their tribulations (Prov 31:6).

Despite the importance of שֵׁכָר, there was no consensus after the Babylonian exile as to what constituted שֵׁכָר. The answers provided to Rabbi Yose's question were (1) while יַיִן refers to wine mixed with water, שֵׁכָר denotes unmixed and therefore stronger wine; and (2) יַיִן constitutes wine that one is religiously obligated to drink, while שֵׁכָר is wine that is optional.[6] Yet elsewhere, the Talmud lists שֵׁכָר as a product brewed from grain.[7] Alternatively, the Targumim, Rashi, Ibn Ezra, and Sefer ha-Mivḥar all understood biblical יַיִן to be 'new wine' (חמר חדת) and שֵׁכָר to be 'old wine' (חמר עתיק).[8] In fact, the meaning of שֵׁכָר and its differences from יַיִן were problematic long before the rabbinic period: the authors of the LXX most often transliterate שֵׁכָר with σικερα.[9]

Today, while 'strong drink' remains the most frequent English translation of שֵׁכָר, confusion about its identity persists. The problem of rendering שֵׁכָר into English is best exemplified by the JPS translation of the Hebrew Bible, which uses ten terms for the single Hebrew word: "liquor," "fermented drink (with footnote 'i.e. wine')," "other liquor," "drink," "strong drink," "any strong drink," "other strong drink," "other intoxicant," "any other intoxicant," and "drunkards (for drinkers of שֵׁכָר)."[10]

---

4. See the similar instructions that Elizabeth receives in Luke 1:15. See also William H. C. Propp, "Was Samuel a Nazirite?" *BR* 14/4 (1999) 2.

5. Note that Ezek 44:21 prohibits wine to those going to the Temple's court. This is both more and less strict than P.

6. Rabbi Eleazar ha-Kappar provides the first explanation in *Num. Rab.* 10:8 (this was subsequently followed by Ramban [*Torah Commentary*]). The latter alternative is put forth by Rabbi Yose.

7. *B. Pesaḥ.* 42a lists Midianite beer (שֵׁכָר הַמָּדִי) among the grain products to be removed from the house for Passover, along with Edomite vinegar (חוֹמֶץ הָאֱדוֹמִי) and Egyptian zythos beer (זִיתוֹם הַמִּצְרִי).

8. For *Tg. Onq., Tg. Ps.-J., Tg. Yer.*, Rashi, Ibn Ezra, and *Sefer ha-Mivḥar*, see Jacob Milgrom, *Numbers* (New York: Jewish Publication Society, 1990) 304 n. 10.

9. Even so, the LXX occasionally translates שֵׁכָר as μεθυσμα 'strong/alcoholic drink' (Judg 13:4, 7, 14; 1 Sam 1:15; Mic 2:11) and μεθη 'intoxicating drink' (Prov 20:1). Yet neither of these terms hints at the ingredients of שֵׁכָר, unlike Greek οινος 'wine' or βρυτος 'beer'. Note the use of σικερα for Hebrew שֵׁכָר in Luke 1:15 and Philo, *On Drunkenness* 138, though Philo later uses μεθυσμα (line 143). Josephus ignores שֵׁכָר, writing that Nazirites must abstain from only wine (*Ant.* 4.72). See also Galenus 19.693.

10. For the JPSV, see "liquor" (Isa 5:11; 24:9; 28:7; 29:9; 56:12; Mic 2:11), "fermented drink" with "wine" footnote (Num 28:7), "other liquor" (Deut 29:5), "drink" (Isa

There exists a disdain for beer in modern scholarship[11] coupled with an exaggerated notion that wine owned a superior status to beer in antiquity.[12]

5:22), "strong drink" (Prov 20:1; 31:6), "any strong drink" (Prov 31:4), "other strong drink" (1 Sam 1:15), "other intoxicant" (Lev 10:9; Deut 14:26; Judg 13:4, 7, 14), "any other intoxicant" (Num 6:3), and "drunkards" (Ps 69:12). Similarly, the NJPSV uses all of these terms with the exception of "other liquor." The KJV uses three terms for the above passages: "strong drink," "strong wine," and "drunkards"; NKJV uses six: "intoxicating drink," "*similar* drink," "similar drink," "drink," "strong drink," and "drunkard." The RSV has the least variation, using only "strong drink" and "drunkards." The NRSV uses "strong drink," "drink," and "drunkards." The JB uses "strong drink," "liquor," and "drunkards."

11. For example, Jack Sasson writes of Melchizedek's offer of bread and wine to Abraham (Gen 14:18), "it would have been uncivilized in that area of antiquity to present any other beverage—beer, water or milk" (Jack M. Sasson, "The Blood of Grapes," *Drinking in Ancient Societies* [ed. Lucio Milano; Padua: Sargon, 1994] 402). More specifically, several authors flagrantly associate wine with civility and beer with loutishness. Thus, Lawrence E. Stager correlates beer-drinking with thuggery and uncouth behavior ("The Impact of the Sea Peoples in Canaan [1185–1050 BCE]," in *The Archaeology of Society in the Holy Land* [ed. Thomas E. Levy; London: Leicester University Press, 1995] 345; "The Fury of Babylon: Ashkelon and the Archaeology of Destruction," *BAR* 22/1 (1996) 64, 68). Stager's negative associations with beer, while clearly exaggerated, seem to be in response to earlier generalizations such as those made by William F. Albright, who claimed textual and archaeological homogeneity in the examination of Philistine material culture, where the abundance of "beer-jugs" fit with the biblical evidence of the Philistines' being "carousers" when compared with the Israelites, especially the teetotaling Nazirite Samson (*The Archaeology of Palestine* [Harmondsworth: Penguin, 1949] 115). Cf. also Jacob Milgrom, *Numbers*, 45. There are also cases in which ancient Near Eastern literature (including *The Epic of Gilgamesh*, the *Enuma Elish*, and Hammurapi's *Law Code*) clearly reference 'beer' (*šikaru*), but scholars chose to translate the term 'wine' or 'strong drink', apparently to avoid degrading the imbibers. See for example *ANET* 66 (*Enuma Elish*), 77 (*Gilgamesh*), and 170 (Hammurapi's *Law Code*).

12. There can be no doubt that ancient Israel loved wine. In evidence of this are the many words for wine in the Hebrew language (John Pairman Brown, "The Mediterranean Vocabulary of the Vine," *VT* 19 [1969] 146–70). According to the Talmud, Israelite exiles said, "Stores of beer in Babylonia are like stores of wine in Palestine" (*b. Pesaḥ.* 8a), and wines from various regions in Israel were famous in antiquity, as they are today (see, for example, Henry F. Lutz, *Viticulture and Brewing in the Ancient Orient* [Leipzig: Hinrichs, 1922] 22–36; Philip Mayerson, "The Use of Ascalon Wine in the Medical Writers of the Fourth to Seventh Centuries," *IEJ* 43 [1993] 169–73). It is also true that wine is more difficult to produce than beer, because viticulture requires permanent fields and social complexity (Lawrence E. Stager, "The Firstfruits of Civilization," in *Palestine in the Bronze and Iron Ages: Papers in Honour of Olga Tufnell* [ed. Jonathan N. Tubb; London: Institute of Archaeology, 1985] 177). Grapes ripen just once a year and only preserve as raisins, which can produce a sweet wine (on raisin wine, see Michal Dayagi-Mendels, *Drink and Be Merry: Wine and Beer in Ancient Times* [Jerusalem: Israel Museum, 1999] 36). Barley and other cereals, however, are easily stored, which allows the production of beer year round. Yet, the fact that ancient Israel produced, consumed, and cherished wine by no means precludes

This, I believe, is partially responsible for the fact that the majority of scholars today, like the rabbinic and targumic authors, believe that שֵׁכָר is most often produced from grapes,[13] or alternatively, dates.[14] Nevertheless, based on textual, ecological, and archaeological arguments, I propose that barley provides the primary fermentable sugar in שֵׁכָר, even though fruits, honey, and spices were frequently added for flavor. Consequently, biblical שֵׁכָר is best understood to be beer.[15]

---

beer production, and the enormous quantities of barley grown in ancient Israel (see below) suggests a wide variety of functions, including brewing.

13. Scholars favoring a grape basis for שֵׁכָר include: Baruch A. Levine, *Numbers 1–20* (AB 4A; New York: Doubleday, 1963) 219–20; Robert P. Teachout, "The Use of Wine in the Old Testament" (Ph.D. diss., Dallas Theological Seminary, 1979) 135, 225, 245–47; Menahem Haran, "נְסָכִים (Libations)," *EncMiq* 5.883–86; Berton Roueché, "Alcohol, I: The Christian Diversion," *New Yorker* (January 9, 1960) 42. Jerome (*Epistulae,* 52.11), however, argued that שֵׁכָר refers to wine and any intoxicating drink, and he is followed by the following scholars: Sasson, "The Blood of Grapes," 400; Manfred Oeming, "שכר," *TWAT* 8.1–5; Milgrom, *Numbers,* 45; Marten Stol, "Beer in Neo-Babylonian Times," in *Drinking in Ancient Societies* (ed. Lucio Milano; Padua: Sargon, 1994) 160; Ephraim Stern, "שֵׁכָר," *EncMiq* 7.677–80. See also the older works of James Death, *The Beer of the Bible: One of the Hitherto Unknown Leavens of Exodus* (London: Trübner, 1887) 56; and George B. Gray, *Numbers* (ICC 4; New York: Scribner's, 1903) 61–62. Others argue that all alcoholic drinks in the Bible were made from grapes, and barley was solely used for bread (Wilfred E. Shewell-Cooper, *Plants, Flowers and Herbs of the Bible* [New Canaan, Conn.: Keats, 1977] 164). See Hans Dieter Betz, "Libation," *ER* 7.537–40, who lists many beverages libated in religion—but not beer—and Michal Dayagi-Mendels, who writes, "In the land of Israel . . . beer was hardly consumed at all" (*Drink and Be Merry,* 113). A minority have translated שֵׁכָר as 'beer', including Richard E. Friedman, *Commentary on the Torah* (San Francisco: Harper San Francisco, 2001) 523; Robert G. Boling, *Judges* (AB 6A; Garden City, N.Y.: Doubleday, 1975) 219–20; Magen Broshi, "Wine in Ancient Palestine," *Israel Museum Journal* 3 (1984) 35; Johann Döller, "Der Wein in Bibel und Talmud," *Bib* 4 (1923) 299; and Werner Dommershausen, "יַיִן," *TWAT* 3.614–20.

14. Lawrence E. Stager, "Ashkelon and the Archaeology of Destruction: Kislev 604 BCE," *ErIsr* 25 (Aviram Volume; 1996) 65*; idem, "The Fury of Babylon," 66; Robert J. Forbes, *Studies in Ancient Technology* (Leiden: Brill, 1955) 3.63; Carey Walsh, *The Fruit of the Vine: Viticulture in Ancient Israel* (HSM 60; Winona Lake, Ind.: Eisenbrauns, 2000) 200–202; Andrew G. Sherratt, "Cups That Cheered," in *Bell Beakers of the Western Mediterranean* (ed. W. H. Waldren and R. C. Kennard; B.A.R. Int. Series 331/1; Oxford: British Archaeological Reports, 1987) 94.

15. In English, from the sixteenth century onward, "beer" is malted barley, water, and hops, while "ale" is simply malted barley and water. Although "ale" would be, in fact, a more exact translation of שֵׁכָר (hops were not used in brewing prior to Medieval times), "beer" has recently become an inclusive term for a variety of undistilled fermented cereal beverages. While beer can be made from wheat, a practice attested in ancient Near Eastern literature, this article will focus solely on the more common form of barley beer.

The Linguistic Case for שֵׁכָר as a Product Brewed Primarily from Barley

There is little doubt that Hebrew שֵׁכָר derives from Akkadian *šikaru* (Sumerian KAŠ) 'barley beer'.[16] The term *šikaru* is widely attested, referencing beer at all of the major Akkadian archival centers, including Alalakh, Amarna, Ebla, Emar, Karana, Mari, Nineveh, Nippur, Nuzi, and Ras Shamra.[17] Eventually the word for "beer" became synonymous with inebriation throughout the ancient Near East, which illustrates beer's magnitude. Thus, in the Hebrew Bible, שׁכר verbally means 'to get drunk'.[18] Similarly, at Ugarit, *škr* is never used nominally as something one drinks but, instead, it is a state that arises from drinking alcohol.[19] In addition to Hebrew and Ugaritic, 'beer' became synonymous with inebriation in Akkadian (*šakāru*), Aramaic (שׁכר), and Arabic (*sakira*).[20] Similarly, in the Egyptian language, 'beer' (*ḥnq*[*t*]) was also used for general drunkenness.[21]

---

16. CAD Š/2 420–28; Wolfram von Soden, *AHw* 1232–33. The identification of *šikaru* with barley beer is based on numerous ancient beer recipes recorded in Akkadian, in which barley and water are the primary ingredients (Civil, "A Hymn to the Beer Goddess and a Drinking Song," 67–89). Residue analysis of ceramics labeled *šikaru* / KAŠ corroborates this (Rudolph H. Michel et al., "The First Wine and Beer: Chemical Detection of Ancient Fermented Beverages," *Analytical Chemistry* 65 [1993] 408a–413a).

17. For references to *šikaru* at all sites, see CAD Š/2 420–28; *AHw* 1232–33. For details of *šikaru* at Mari and Karana, see Stephanie Dalley, *Mari and Karana* (New York: Longman, 1984) 89. On Nippur, see Danielle Deheselle, "La bière en Babylonie selon des tablettes économiques kassites de Nippur," *Akkadica* 86 (1994) 24–38. Note also *šikaru* and barley (*šeʾu*) as staples of hospitality in the Amarna Letters (Jørgen A. Knudtzon, *Die El-Amarna-Tafeln* [Leipzig: Hinrichs, 1915] 55:11; 161:22; 324:13; 325:16; 1522). See also George Giacumakis, *The Akkadian of Alalaḫ* (Paris: Mouton, 1970) 104. Ugarit imported *šikaru* from Crete (RS 16.238 lines 1–11; A. Bernard Knapp, "Spice, Drugs, Grain and Grog: Organic Goods in Bronze Age East Mediterranean Trade," in *Bronze Age Trade in the Mediterranean* [ed. N. H. Gale; Studies in Mediterranean Archaeology 90; Jonsered, Sweden: Åströms, 1991] 37).

18. E.g., Gen 9:21; 43:34; 2 Sam 11:13; Isa 29:9; Jer 25:27. The root is also used adjectivally (1 Sam 1:13; 25:36; 1 Kgs 16:9; Isa 28:1, 3; Joel 1:5).

19. Thus, El, on a particularly intense binder, drinks 'wine until satiety, new wine to drunkenness' (*yn ʿd šbʿ trt ʿd škr*) in *KTU* 1.114.3–4 and 16. Similarly in the Aqhat Epic (*KTU* 1.17.I.30; II.5, 19–20), one of the jobs of devout children is to "take dad's hand when he is drunk (*bškrn*), bear him up when full of wine (*šbʿ*[*t*] *yn*)." Similarly, wine-drinking is paralleled to drunkenness in Joel 1:5 and Isa 24:9.

20. For Akkadian, see CAD Š/2 157. For Aramaic, see Michael Sokoloff, *A Dictionary of Jewish Palestinian Aramaic of the Byzantine Period* (Ramat-Gan: Bar Ilan University Press, 1990) 551. For Arabic, see Edward W. Lane, *Arabic-English Lexicon* (London: William & Norgate, 1872) 4.1390–91.

21. Adolf Erman and Hermann Grapow, *Wörterbuch der Ägyptischen Sprache* (Leipzig: Hinrichs, 1929) 3.117–18, 169.

In the Hebrew Bible, nominal שֵׁכָר is attested 20 times, and in all but one of these (Num 28:7) it stands in parallel to "wine."[22] Both wine and שֵׁכָר are alcoholic beverages, so their parallelism in poetry would be expected. Yet, the parallel use of wine and שֵׁכָר in prose dictates that somehow שֵׁכָר is different from ordinary יַיִן.

Both terms are common in extrabiblical documents that inventory wine and beer, as well as literature that records the two beverages consumed in tandem. For example, a palace record of Ashurnasirpal II refers to participants feasting on 10,000 measures of beer (*šikaru*) and the same of wine.[23] In a Neo-Assyrian wine magazine found at Calah, excavators found 11 tablets concerned with the distribution of wine and beer (*šikaru*).[24] Similarly, at Ashkelon, a late seventh-century B.C.E. ostracon inventories units of red wine (יין אדם) and units of שכר.[25] The same phenomenon happens in Aramaic and Egyptian documents, where record-keepers tabulated quantities of beer and wine.[26] The same pairing appears often in ancient Near Eastern

---

22. In Num 28:7 שֵׁכָר is used alone. Other nominal usages of שֵׁכָר include: Lev 10:9; Num 6:3 (bis); Deut 14:26; 29:6; Judg 13:4, 7, 14; 1 Sam 1:15; Isa 5:11, 22; 24:9; 28:7; 29:9; 56:12; Mic 2:11; Prov 20:1; 31:4, 6.

23. Donald J. Wiseman, "A New Stela of Aššur-naṣir-pal II," *Iraq* 14 (1952) 24–44.

24. J. V. Kinnier Wilson, *The Nimrud Wine Lists* (London: British School of Archaeology in Iraq, 1972) 81.

25. However, Lawrence E. Stager believes that here שכר refers to date-wine, citing date-wine in Syriac as *šakrā'* and the site's sandy soil as better inclined for viticulture and palms than barley (Lawrence E. Stager, "The Impact of the Sea Peoples in Canaan [1185–1050 BCE]," 345; idem, "The Fury of Babylon: Ashkelon and the Archaeology of Destruction," 64, 68). However, barley thrives within two kilometers of Ashkelon as the seaside dunes are replaced by excellent soil. Furthermore, remains of Bronze and Iron Age barley have been found at Ashkelon (personal communication with Mordechai Kislev), and a seventh-century B.C.E. ostracon from Ashkelon refers to either the import or export of cereal (Frank M. Cross, Jr., "A Philistine Ostracon from Ashkelon," *BAR* 22/1 [1996] 64–65). Also note that in the late nineteenth century, Gaza (15 km south of Ashkelon) exported massive amounts of barley to England for beer manufacturing (Georg Gatt, "Industrielles aus Gaza," *ZDPV* 8 [1885] 69–79; Martin A. Meyer, *History of the City of Gaza* [New York: Columbia University Press, 1907] 107).

26. On the parallel usage in Aramaic documents, see Godfrey R. Driver, *Aramaic Documents of the Fifth Century B.C.* (Oxford: Clarendon, 1957) 6.3; and Judah B. Segal, *Aramaic Texts from North Saqqâra* (London: Egypt Exploration Society, 1983) 42.3–4, and possibly in 20.2; 81.6. On the parallel mention of "beer" and "wine" in Egyptian documents, note Mu-Chou Poo, *Wine and Wine Offering in the Religion of Ancient Egypt* (London: Kegan Paul, 1995) 30–34; and Leonard H. Lesko, *King Tut's Wine Cellar* (Berkeley: B. C. Scribe, 1977) 27–29. Note also that barley and grapes are frequently paired in ancient literature (e.g., Joel 1:11–12).

literature. The gods in the *Enuma Elish* drink beer (*šikaru*), wine (*karanu*), and sweet-beer (*matkiu*) all in one sitting.[27]

Starting in the Neo-Babylonian period, Akkadian *šikaru* began occasionally to refer to an alcoholic beverage in which dates served as the primary sugars.[28] However, given that diet remains among the most conservative aspects in any culture's evolution, it seems unlikely that the ancient Israelites or the authors of the Hebrew Bible would have adopted the Neo-Babylonian *culinarius* or its terminology. A temporal issue forms a larger hurdle for those who claim biblical שֵׁכָר was date-wine. Certain biblical references to שֵׁכָר, such as Mic 2:11 and Isa 5:11, 22; 24:9; 28:7; and 29:9 were composed in the eighth century B.C.E., long before *šikaru* as date-wine would likely have infiltrated Israelite culture. Etymologically and contextually, Hebrew שֵׁכָר is best identified with beer.[29]

Mixed Drinks and Terminology

Compounding the difficulty in identifying שֵׁכָר is the fact that beverages in antiquity most often contained many ingredients; products solely composed of barley, grapes, or dates were rare.[30] Dates were among the most frequent additives to beer,[31] though other fruits (especially grapes, sycamore,

---

27. *Enuma Elish*, III.134–36. Note also the frequent depictions of gods with both grapes and cereals (Charles Seltman, *Wine in the Ancient World* [London: Routledge & Kegan Paul, 1957] 27–31, 156).

28. Marten Stol, "Beer in Neo-Babylonian Times," 155–83.

29. In fact, there were a limited number of alcoholic beverages prior to the invention of distilled spirits in the Middle Ages. On distillation and distilled spirits, see Alfred Lucas, *Ancient Egyptian Materials and Industries* (4th ed.; J. R. Harris; London: Edward Arnold, 1962) 24.

30. See Mary Ann Murray, "Viticulture and Wine Production," in *Ancient Egyptian Materials and Technology* (ed. Paul T. Nicholson and Ian Shaw; Cambridge: Cambridge University Press, 2000) 592.

31. On beer mixed with dates, see the excellent article by Stol, "Beer in Neo-Babylonian Times," 155–83, though he is too quick to isolate dates and barley from composite beverages such as mixed date beer, at times called 'prime beer' (*šikaru rēštû*). As Stol himself points out, in the Hymn to Ninkasi, the beer goddess includes 'honey and wine' (làl geštin) in the mash. For further information on dates and beer, see Civil, "A Hymn to the Beer Goddess and a Drinking Song," 70, line 36; also relevant is the Sumerian poem *Enki's Return to Nippur*, where the brewer pours date-syrup (làl-zú.lum.ma) into the beer malt (A. J. Ferrara, *Nanna-Suen's Journey to Nippur* [Rome: Pontifical Biblical Institute, 1973] 123–24); and Paul-Alain Beaulieu, "The Brewers of Nippur," *JCS* 47 (1995) 85–96, where dates are listed as ingredients for beer along with barley. Date beer is also frequently listed in Egyptian documents; see Charles F. Nims, "The Bread and Beer Problems of the Moscow Mathematical Papyrus," *JEA* 44 (1958) 60–65; William J. Darby, Paul Ghalioungui,

and figs), honey (fruit and bee), and spices were also common.[32] Similarly, wine was often flavored with a variety of items, including dates, pomegranates, figs, terebinth, honey (fruit and bee), egg whites, and crushed barley.[33] There are also ample cases in which beer and wine products were mixed together and then consumed.[34] However, as a general rule, the drinks are best

and Louis Grivetti, *Food: The Gift of Osiris* (London: Academic, 1977) 543–47; David M. Dixon, "A Note on Cereals in Ancient Egypt," in *The Domestication and Exploitation of Plants and Animals* (ed. Peter J. Ucko and Geoffrey W. Dimbleby; Chicago: Aldine, 1969) 139. Wolfgang Helck says the Egyptian ratio for one beer of barley, dates, and wheat was 2:2:1, based on court records (*Das Bier im Alten Ägypten* [Berlin: Institut für Gärungsgewerbe und Biotechnologie, 1971] 33). For the same mixture, later, in Gaul, see Athenaeus, *Deipnosophists*, 152c.

32. Delwen Samuel, "Brewing and Baking," in *Ancient Egyptian Materials and Technology* (ed. Paul T. Nicholson and Ian Shaw; Cambridge: Cambridge University Press, 2000) 547–50; Helck, *Das Bier im Alten Ägypten*, 15–42; W. Röllig, *Das Bier im alten Mesopotamien* (Berlin: Gesellschaft für die Geschichte und Bibliographie des Brauwesens, 1970) 28–43. Pomegranates and aniseed-flavored barley beer at Mari (Dalley, *Mari and Karana*, 89). On aromatic herbs in *bappir* (beer bread), see Benno Landsberger and Oliver R. Gurney, "Practical Vocabulary of Assur," *AfO* 18 (1957–58) 337. Note that *b. Bat.* 96b says people consumed beers of plain barley as well as barley flavored with figs and blackberries (see also *b. Pesaḥ.* 107a).

33. See Broshi, "Wine in Ancient Palestine," 26–27; Lutz, *Viticulture and Brewing in the Ancient Orient*, 17–18; Dayagi-Mendels, *Drink and Be Merry*, 36–37. On honey mixed with wine, see "*dišpu*," CAD D 161–63; cf. the mixture of wine and honey at Ugarit (*KTU* 1.14.IV.1–2). Date-flavored wine is mentioned in the Tosefta (*Ma'aś. Š.* 2.4) and by Pliny (*Natural History* 14.19), who also mentions wines of figs, pomegranates, and other fruits (*NH* 8.5). Wine is mixed with milk and honey in Euripides, *Bacchae* 142. Several wines in early dynastic Egypt contained figs and grapes (Patrick E. McGovern et al., "The Beginnings of Winemaking and Viniculture in the Ancient Near East and Egypt," *Expedition* 39/1 [1997] 10; Patrick E. McGovern, "Wine for Eternity," *Archaeology* 51/4 [1998] 28–34). A sixth-century B.C.E. inscription from Lachish mentions raisin-wine, referred to as 'black raisin juice' (מיץ צמקם שחרת). Raisins have also been discovered near many drinking vessels (Dayagi-Mendels, *Drink and Be Merry*, 36). On terebinth-resin in wine, see Pliny, *NH* 14.57, 92, 107, 112, 131, 134; Patrick E. McGovern, "Wine of Egypt's Golden Age," *JEA* 83 (1997) 84–89. Egg whites were added according to the Mishnah (*Šabb.* 20:2). On barley mixed into wine, along with goat cheese, see Homer, *Iliad* 11.638–39 and *Odyssey* 10.234.

34. Beer and wine were mixed together and then consumed in Gaul (Athenaeus, *Deipnosophists* 152c) and in Phrygia (Patrick E. McGovern et al., "A Funerary Feast Fit for King Midas," *Nature* 402 [December 23, 1999] 863–64; John Fleischman, "Midas' Feast," *Discover* 21/11 [2000] 70–75; Stephanie Pain, "Grog of the Greeks," *New Scientist* 164/2214 [1999] 54–57). Wine mixed with beer was also used in enemas (Darby et al., *Food: The Gift of Osiris*, 484–85). Other medicinal attestations include the mixture of barley, wine, and honey that were offered to snakes so as to avoid bites from asps (Aelian 3.17.5). Perhaps the mixture of beer and wine relates to Isa 5:22, where wine is drunk, but שכר is mixed (מסך), though the traditional understanding of mixing wine and beer with water seems likely (cf.

identified by their primary fermentable sugars: fruits for wine, and cereals for beer.

An occasional interchange of terminology related to wine and beer further hampers conclusive identification. There are times in Semitic languages when viticultural terms are used for barley products. Thus, Arabic _khamr_ is used for the alcoholic products of either grapes or barley.[35] One text from Emar glosses _šikaru_MEŠ _karānu_ 'beer-wine' with _ḫa-am-[ra]_, a term most often associated with wine.[36] Similarly in the Greek language, beer is at times referred to as 'barley wine' (κριθινος οινος).[37] While less common, cases exist where words for 'beer' are used for wine. Thus in Akkadian, wine is at times deemed _šikar šadî_ 'mountain beer', due to the location of the grapes.[38]

Nevertheless, it must be remembered that the interchange of terminology is rare, and in the overwhelming majority of cases in the ancient Near East, the root _škr_ refers to a product composed primarily of barley. The probable referent of biblical שֵׁכָר is thus beer, unless demonstrated otherwise.

A Grape-Based שֵׁכָר? Nazirites, Viticultural Hendiadys, and the Nature of Fermentation

The primary biblical evidence for a grape-based שֵׁכָר relies on two passages that detail the Nazirite's abstentions:

---

other passages in which wine is mixed [מסך]: Isa 65:11; Ps 75:9; Ps 102:10; Prov 23:30; 9:2, 5). See Brown, "The Mediterranean Vocabulary of the Vine," 146–70. Beverages composed of barley and grapes seem to be textually attested in Akkadian, if we read _šikaru karānu_ 'beer-wine' this way.

35. Arent J. Wensinck, "khamr: Juridical Aspects," _The Encyclopaedia of Islam_ (new ed.; Leiden: Brill, 1978) 4.994–97.

36. Emar 369, line 38. See Daniel E. Fleming, _The Installation of Baal's High Priestess at Emar_ (HSS 42; Atlanta: Scholars Press, 1992) 39, 142–45. See also Itamar Singer, _The Hittite KI.LAM-Festival_ (Studien zu den Bogazköy-Texten 27; Wiesbaden: Harrassowitz, 1983) 1.157 and n. 25; Joan Goodnick Westenholz, _Cuneiform Inscriptions in the Collection of the Bible Lands Museum Jerusalem: The Emar Tablets_ (Groningen: Styx, 2000) 62. Perhaps Hos 3:2 is also relevant. While the MT reads that Hosea purchases Gomer for 15 shekels of silver, a homer of barley (חמר שׁערים), and a measure of barley (לֵתֶךְ שׁערים), the LXX renders the final item 'skin of wine' (νεβελ οινου), raising the possibility that some understood חמר שׁערים as 'barley-wine.' The combination of produce from grain and vine fits nicely with other passages in Hosea (e.g., 2:8–9, 22; 7:14; 9:2).

37. Henry G. Liddell and Robert Scott, _A Greek-English Lexicon_ (9th rev. ed.; Oxford: Clarendon, 1968) 995. See, for example, Polybius, _History_ (34.9.15).

38. CAD Š/1 54; Jean Bottéro, "Le vin dans une civilsation de la bière: La Mésopotamie," in _In Vino Veritas_ (ed. Oswyn Murray and Manuela Tecusçan; London: British School at Rome, 1995) 21–34; Jane M. Renfrew, "Vegetables in the Ancient Near Eastern Diet," in _Civilizations of the Ancient Near East_ (ed. Jack M. Sasson; New York: Scribner's, 1995) 1.191–202. Note also the combined terms _karānu šikaru_ 'wine beer' and _šikaru karānu_ 'beer wine' (CAD Š/2 428).

1. He shall separate from wine and שֵׁכָר, he shall not drink wine vinegar and שֵׁכָר vinegar; and he shall not drink all grape juice (מִשְׁרַת עֲנָבִים), and he shall not eat grapes, fresh nor dried. All the days of his separation; from all that is made from the grapevine of wine he shall not eat, from seeds (מֵחַרְצַנִּים) to skins (זָג).

(Num 6:3–4)

2. You will not eat from all that comes from the vine of wine and you may not drink wine and שֵׁכָר.

(Judg 13:14)

In the first passage, the priestly author elaborates on the term עֲנָבִים, ensuring that the Nazirite cannot consume any part of the fruit until after his term of consecration, when he may drink wine (Num 6:20).[39] Some scholars argue that this elaboration on grapes and their products suggests a grape basis for both wine and שֵׁכָר.[40] Yet nowhere does the text say שֵׁכָר is composed of grapes. The detailed prohibitions of grapes are merisms, reading "fresh nor dried" and "from seeds to skins" to refer to all stages and all parts of the fruit. Similarly, the second passage (Judg 13:14) does not claim that שֵׁכָר is composed of grapes; rather, the Nazirite, and in this case, his pregnant mother, must not consume wine or any grape product, and she must also abstain from imbibing שֵׁכָר.

The issue in both passages is the avoidance of fermented liquids. Relevant here is the complex procedure by which barley and wheat are converted to alcohol. Following the cereal harvest, the initial stage in beer production involves malting. Malting is achieved by adding moisture to the grains and allowing them to germinate, chemically unleashing diastatic enzymes that cause the hydrolysis of starches to maltose. Subsequently, the malted kernels are ground and then heated for a short time, allowing enzymes further to break down the starches into fermentable sugars, a procedure called "mashing," whose end-product is "wort."[41] Finally, yeast is added to the wort, and after a few days the fermentable maltose sugars are converted to alcohol.

39. Note the similar stipulation by Plutarch (*Quaestiones Romanae* 112) that the Roman high priest could neither drink wine nor come into contact with vines.

40. See for example Levine, *Numbers 1–20*, 219–21; George F. Moore, *Judges* (ICC; New York: Scribner's, 1910) 316–17; Gray, *Numbers*, 61–63.

41. On the procedure of making beer in antiquity, see primarily Samuel, "Brewing and Baking," 537–76. See also Marvin A. Powell, "Metron Ariston," in *Drinking in Ancient Societies* (ed. Lucio Milano; Padua: Sargon, 1994) 91–119; Röllig, *Das Bier im alten Mesopotamien*, 28–63; Hildegard Lewy, "Miscellanea Nuziana II," *Or* 28 (1959) 118–19 n. 2; Louis F. Hartman and A. Leo Oppenheim, *On Beer and Brewing Techniques in Ancient Mesopotamia* (JAOSSup 10; Baltimore: American Oriental Society, 1950); Civil, "A Hymn to the Beer Goddess and a Drinking Song," 67–89.

Thus, there is no chance of contacting alcohol by eating cereal products made from unmalted barley and/or wheat. In fact, the only cereal product other than beer that runs the risk of containing alcohol is leaven, a commodity heavily legislated.[42]

Contrasted to this are grapes, whose natural state incorporates sugar and water. All that is needed to ferment the liquid is yeast, which can be either airborne or inherent to the "bloom" on the fruit's skin.[43] Consequently, grape products are easily fermentable, and freshly squeezed grape juice (תִּירוֹשׁ) as well as overripe grapes still on the vine often contain alcohol.[44] Thus, the details concerning abstention from grapes in the above passages are necessary because, while the preconsecrated Nazirite can eat bread without risk, to maintain ritual purity he/she must avoid not only שֵׁכָר and wine but all products from grapes. Thus, the viticultural elaboration in Num 6:3–4 and Judg 13:14 does not confine שֵׁכָר to the vine.

Barley's Magnitude

Barley is one of the most frequently grown, highest yielding, widely diverse, and archaeologically abundant plants in the ancient Near East and in Israel in particular. Wild barley (*Hordeum spontaneum*) extends throughout the Fertile Crescent and has been harvested from the Paleolithic period until today.[45] Barley has a wider tolerance to various environments than do emmer and einkorn wheat.[46] It is more adaptive to salinized soils as well as drought

---

42. On leaven (שְׂאֹר), see Heinrich F. Beck, "Leaven," *IDB* 3.104–5. Also of interest is Pliny's description (*NH* 18.26) and Death, *The Beer of the Bible*, 11–68. Note also that beer and beer vinegar must be removed from the house during Passover according to the Talmud (*b. Pesaḥ.* 3.1).

43. Ján Farkaš, *Technology and Biochemistry of Wine* (New York: Gordon and Breach Science, 1988) 1.171–237.

44. Even תִּירוֹשׁ seems to be fermented in Hos 4:11.

45. Fred Wendorf and Romuald Schild, "The Use of Ground Grain during the Late Paleolithic of the Lower Nile Valley, Egypt," in *Origins of African Plant Domestication* (ed. Jack R. Harlan et al.; Paris: Mouton, 1976) 269–88; Daniel Zohary and Maria Hopf, *Domestication of Plants in the Old World: The Origin and Spread of Cultivated Plants in West Asia, Europe, and the Nile Valley* (Oxford: Clarendon, 1988) 52–63; Douglas J. Brewer, Donald B. Redford, and Susan Redford, *Domestic Plants and Animals: The Egyptian Origins* (Warminster: Aris & Phillips, 1998) 27; Karl W. Butzer, "Agricultural Origins in the Near East as a Geographical Problem," in *Prehistoric Agriculture* (ed. Stuart Struever; Garden City, N.Y.: Natural History, 1971) 209–35; Thomas W. Kavanagh, "Archaeological Parameters for the Beginnings of Beer," *Brewing Techniques* 2/5 (1994) 44–51.

46. Brewer et al., *Domestic Plants and Animals*, 24–31. Barley is more tolerant to inclement conditions, including heat, and barley produces more reliable yields than wheat (Marvin A. Powell, "Salt, Seeds and Yields in Sumerian Agriculture," *ZA* 75 [1985] 7–38).

and extreme heat than other cereals.[47] It is for this reason that it was one of the very first plants to be domesticated[48] and continues to be grown in abundance, even in the deserts of Jordan and Israel.[49]

Several Syro-Palestinian inscriptions mention barley, including the tenth-century B.C.E. Gezer Calendar, which chronicles the 'month for harvesting barley' (ירח קצר שערם).[50] Sinuhe mentions barley as part of the bounty of the land of Ya, thought to be Canaan.[51] Barley's significance is also attested in the art-historical record, where it frequently represents the land's fertility.[52] Re-

---

47. Brewer et al., *Domestic Plants and Animals*, 26; Zohary and Hopf, *Domestication of Plants in the Old World*, 55, 60; Michael Zohary, *Plants of the Bible* (Cambridge: Cambridge University Press, 1982) 76; Oded Borowski, *Agriculture in Iron Age Israel* (Winona Lake, Ind.: Eisenbrauns, 1987) 92. Barley is also grown in Egypt after taking back land that was used to make salt (Vivi Täckholm and Mohammed Drar, *Flora of Egypt* [Cairo: Cairo University Press] 1.284).

48. Barley's early domestication was known to Pliny (*NH* 18.4). Homer calls barley "the marrow of men" (*Odyssey* 20.108). On barley's early history, see Jack R. Harlan and Daniel Zohary, "Distribution of Wild Wheats and Barley," *Science* 153 (1966) 1074–80; Zohary, *Plants of the Bible*, 76.

49. Avinoam Danin, *Desert Vegetation of Israel and Sinai* (Jerusalem: Cana, 1983) 54. Barley, it seems, owns a history of popularity followed by disdain. Thus, during the Roman period, barley became the cereal of the poor and of animals, though prior to this it was consumed by all classes (Peter Garnsey, *Food and Society in Classical Antiquity* [Cambridge: Cambridge University Press, 1999] 17–21; 119–20). Similarly, barley was the main cereal of the Old and Middle Kingdoms in Egypt, while emmer supplanted its popularity in the New Kingdom (Brewer et al., *Domestic Plants and Animals*, 28). Herodotus claims that barley is "a disgraceful food among the Egyptians" (*History* 2.36), though Athenaeus 600 years later writes that it was esteemed (*Deipnosophists* 3:114d).

50. See P. Kyle McCarter, "The Gezer Calendar," *COS* (ed. William W. Hallo; Leiden: Brill, 2000) 2.222; William F. Albright, "The Gezer Calendar," *BASOR* 92 (1943) 16–26; *ANET*, 320. The vernal ripening of barley in early May/late April corresponds to the Hebrew Bible, which refers to barley's fruition a few weeks before wheat (Exod 9:31; Josh 3:15; Ruth 2:23; cf. John 6). For the eighth-century B.C.E. "barley letter" from Samaria, see Eleazar L. Sukenik, "Inscribed Hebrew and Aramaic Potsherds from Samaria," *PEQ* (1933) 152–56; William F. Albright, "Ostracon C 1101 of Samaria," *PEQ* (1936) 211–15; *ANET*, 321. For other inscriptions mentioning barley, see Jacob Hoftijzer and Karl Jongeling, *Dictionary of the North-West Semitic Inscriptions* (Leiden, Brill, 1995) 2.1180; Borowski, *Agriculture in Iron Age Israel*, 91–92.

51. Miriam Lichtheim, *Ancient Egyptian Literature* (Berkeley: University of California Press, 1975) 1.226; *ANET*, 19. On the location of Ya, see Benjamin Mazar, "Canaan on the Threshold of the Age of the Patriarchs," *ErIsr* 3 (Cassuto Volume; 1954) 25 [Hebrew]; Anson F. Rainey, "The World of Sinuhe," *IOS* 2 (1972) 376. Egypt imported barley from the Levant (Darby et al., *Food: The Gift of Osiris*, 482). Note that barley (κριθή) production along with wheat and viticulture are the signs of civilization in Homer's *Odyssey* 9.110, 12.112.

52. See, for example, the coins of Agrippa I (r. 41–44 B.C.E.) in Arie Kindler, *Coins of*

mains of barley in Iron Age strata are widely attested in the Syro-Palestinian archaeological record. For example, more than one ton of burned barley was found in chamber three of the Iron Age gate at Bethsaida.[53]

Similarly, the Hebrew Bible records barley (שְׂעֹרָה) as one of the most abundant and important crops of ancient Israel. It is one of the seven species by which the Promised Land is blessed (Deut 8:8). In fact, it was so common that its price was approximately half that of wheat (2 Kgs 7:1, 16, 18; cf. Rev 6:6),[54] and the value of a field was determined by the amount of barley required to sow it (Lev 27:16). Vast quantities of barley were allegedly needed to maintain Solomon's palace economy, because barley paid the Temple workers (2 Chr 2:9) and fed his 40,000 horses (1 Kgs 4:28). Barley also had a cultic function, since it was frequently offered to Yahweh (Lev 27:16; Num 5:15; cf. Lev 23:10–14).[55] Thus there is no doubt that ancient Israel, like its neighbors, planted, harvested, and consumed mass quantities of barley. The Hebrew Bible attests to barley's being eaten raw (2 Kgs 4:42), parched (2 Sam 17:28), and perhaps in porridge (Ezek 4:9).[56] Barley was ground into flour (Num 5:15) and baked into bread (Judg 7:13; Ezek 4:12). It was also used as animal feed (1 Kgs 2:28).[57] Admittedly, there is no direct textual evidence in

---

the *Land of Israel* (Jerusalem: Keter, 1974) 41–42. For extrabiblical depictions, see *ANEP*, 464, 614.

53. Rami Arav, Richard A. Freund, and John F. Schroeder Jr., "Bethsaida Rediscovered," *BAR* 26/1 (2000) 53. On the connection between grain and gates, note 1 Kgs 22:10 and Aqhat (*KTU* 1.17.V.7). Barley has also been found in Iron Age strata at Afula, Khirbet Abu Tabaq, Beer-sheba, and Arad (Borowski, *Agriculture in Iron Age Israel*, 92). Also note that more than four tons of barley was discovered at Late Bronze Boğazköy-Ḫattuša, which had storage facilities for over 6,000 tons of grain (Jürgen Seeher, "Current Archaeological Research at Bogazköy," Lecture, March 29, 2001 at Ben-Gurion University of the Negev).

54. See Philip Mayerson, "Grain Prices in Late Antiquity and the Nature of the Evidence," in *Solving Riddles and Untying Knots: Biblical, Epigraphic, and Semitic Studies in Honor of Jonas C. Greenfield* (ed. Z. Zevit, S. Gitin, and M. Sokoloff; Winona Lake, Ind.: Eisenbrauns, 1995) 443–49.

55. Barley was also offered to Egyptian and Mesopotamian gods (Darby et al., *Food: The Gift of Osiris*, 481–83) and was a common offering in the Greco-Roman world (Garnsey, *Food and Society in Classical Antiquity*, 119). Furthermore, barley's germination was connected with notions of rebirth in the afterlife, as it was planted in Osiris-shaped boxes packed with silt from the Nile found in many New Kingdom Tombs, including Tutankamon's (Dixon, "A Note on Cereals in Ancient Egypt," 131–42).

56. Cf. Pliny, *NH* 18.14.

57. It is unknown what portion of the harvested cereals in ancient Israel would have been designated for beer production. Compare the Middle Ages in Europe, in which an estimated 20–30% of the cereal crop was used to produce beer (Sherratt, "Cups That Cheered," 95), although some estimate that 40% was used for beer in ancient Mesopotamia (Rivka Gonen, *Grain: Dagon Collection* [Jerusalem: Shikmona, 1979] 54).

the Hebrew Bible linking barley to שֵׁכָר.[58] But if ancient Israel did not drink beer, their abstention was unique in the entire ancient Near East.[59]

Conclusion

Rabbi Yose's question concerning the difference between wine and שֵׁכָר in the Hebrew Bible can now be answered. The conflation of evidence from linguistic and archaeological sources supports the identification of biblical שֵׁכָר with beer brewed primarily from barley. The ancient Israelites, like their neighbors, produced, consumed, and enjoyed beer.[60]

58. Concerning a possible reference to beer production and consumption in Qoh 11:1–2, in which the author advises one to "throw your bread into the water," see my "Beer Production by Throwing Bread into Water: A New Interpretation of Qoh. XI 1–2," *VT* 52 (2002) 275–78.

59. Note that beer was a large industry in third-century B.C.E. Amman/Philadelphia as noted in Zenon's letters 59199–202 (Campbell C. Edgar, *Zenon Papyri* [New York: Olms, 1971] 2.59–62).

60. I wish to thank William H. C. Propp (University of California, San Diego), Richard E. Friedman (University of California, San Diego), and Delwen Samuel (University College London) for their valuable comments on previous drafts of this article. I would like to express my gratitude to the American Schools of Oriental Research, the United States Information Agency, and the W. F. Albright Institute of Archaeological Research for funding this project.

Chapter 4
Whom Did Cain Raise?
Redaction and J's Primeval History

RISA LEVITT KOHN

The effect of the Flood on humanity in the Priestly source (P) signifies a new beginning, articulated in a divinely initiated covenant. But in J, the deluge appears to have little effect on humanity. Yahweh promises to refrain from cursing the ground by reiterating humanity's evil inclinations (Gen 8:21). Then, a drunken, naked Noah curses his own son. Lamech's three sons, founders of the arts of civilization, perish in the Flood and are apparently supplanted by Noah's three sons. Noah, from the line that had "begun to call on the name of Yahweh" (Gen 4:26), survives but carries with him the evil state of humanity that initially led to the deluge.

Wellhausen viewed J's Flood as an "isolated piece" without connection to the rest of the J narrative.[1] He identified two distinct layers within the Yahwist's primeval history. The first contains the Flood account and the Table of Nations in Genesis 10; the second knows nothing of the Flood and contains the remaining passages traditionally assigned to J's primeval history. He noted that J's Flood narrative disagrees with both what precedes and what follows it. Gen 4:16–24 identifies Jabal, Jubal, and Tubal Cain as inaugurators of a new epoch after the Eden episode, wherein all of humanity is divided into craft guilds. According to Wellhausen, this reflects the "present situation" of the author and not one that has been or will be destroyed by the Flood.

Author's note: The seed for this paper was sown in the fall of 1990. As a graduate student at UCSD, I was discussing with David Noel Freedman J's Flood narrative and the ways it had been dissected by source critics. Not one of these scholars seemed ready to accept that J's Flood narrative fit with the rest of the source. Noel suggested I "look into it." I have ended up doing just that, on and off, ever since. Noel has entertained each new theory or observation with enthusiasm and insightful discussion, shaping and refining my work along the way. It is for this reason, with great gratitude and admiration, that I dedicate the following paper to my teacher.

1. Wellhausen, *Prolegomena zur Geschichte Israels* (5th ed.; Berlin: Reimer, 1899) 319–21.

In contrast, J's Flood account and the Table of Nations place Noah at the beginning of history. Here, humanity is divided into nations originating from his sons, Shem, Ham, and Japhet. Wellhausen noted that this, too, describes the "present civilization." This information, however, contradicts that of Gen 4:16–24. Taking Wellhausen's lead, numerous scholars have proposed their own theories in an effort to smooth out J's apparent inconsistencies. At least seven separate theories have been suggested. Additional J "layers" have been uncovered, including an anthropomorphic layer, an archaic layer, a postexilic layer, and a non-Israelite layer. Each proposal is a little more complex than the one preceding it.[2]

Recent scholarship emphasizes the unity of J, yet the preceding issues remain without explanation. What is the function of the Flood in J's narrative? What is the relationship between Lamech and his sons and Noah and his sons? Specifically, what is Noah's connection to Lamech and to the Flood in J?

In order to answer these questions, we will find it instructive to examine briefly the Priestly writer's version of the Primeval History. In P, creation is a cosmic event in which God speaks the universe into being, transforming chaos into order. Humanity is created in "God's image" and is blessed with the task of multiplying and filling the earth.

The essence of this narrative is reiterated in the genealogical list of Genesis 5, which begins with the day of humanity's creation and restates that male and female were created in the image of God and that they were blessed on the day of creation (Gen 5:1–2; cf. Gen 1:27–28). Humanity's preliminary fulfillment of the command to be fruitful and multiply is realized in Gen 5:3, where Adam fathers a son in *his* own image. Adam genealogically imparts the divine image and blessing to his son Seth.[3] The rest of the genealogy extends this transmission through a series of firstborn sons, ending with Lamech (5:28).[4] P's list resumes in 5:31–32, where the genealogy splits into three with Noah's sons, Shem, Ham, and Japhet.

The Priestly writer then introduces his Flood account. The impetus for the Flood in P is recounted in Gen 6:11–12: "The earth was corrupt before

2. See, for example, B. Stade, "Beiträge zur Pentateuchkritik," *ZAW* 14 (1894) 265–300; H. Gunkel, *Legends of Genesis* (Chicago: Open Court, 1901) 124; J. Skinner, *Genesis* (New York: Scribner's, 1910); R. Pfeiffer, *Introduction to the Old Testament* (New York: Harper, 1941) 159–67; O. Eissfeldt, *The Old Testament: An Introduction* (German, 1934; Harper & Row: New York, 1965) 194; G. Fohrer, *Einletung in das Alte Testament* (Quelle & Meyer: Heidelberg, 1969) 159–64.

3. Cf. R. R. Wilson, *Geneaology and History in the Biblical World* (New Haven: Yale University Press, 1977) 164.

4. The reference in this list to Noah in Gen 5:29 is generally read as a Yahwistic fragment within P's genealogy—it contains an etymological etiology similar to those found in J and obviously interrupts the genealogical pattern established in P. See further below.

God, and the earth was filled with violence. And God looked upon the earth, and here it was corrupt because all flesh had corrupted its way on the earth." Not just humanity but all of creation is corrupt according to P. Destruction is brought about by means of cosmic waters (7:11), returning the world to the precreation state originally described in Genesis 1.[5] Noah and his family are singled out to survive the Flood, ostensibly because of Noah's righteousness (Gen 6:9). P then recommissions Noah, using language identical to that of Genesis 1, "Be fruitful, multiply and fill the earth." The postflood world is thus a new beginning articulated in and guaranteed by a divinely initiated covenant (Gen 9:1). P's primeval history concludes with a second genealogical list, extending from Noah's sons through Abraham.

Contrast the situation according to J. After the creation of the universe, we have the story of the first humans. The narrative begins with Adam and Eve in "Eden at the east" (Gen 2:8). Yahweh confronts the pair after they have eaten from the forbidden tree. He punishes both of them. The woman will suffer pain during childbirth and will long for her husband. The man will have to work the land for food, but the land will be cursed (Gen 3:17). Man and Woman are then expelled from the garden (Gen 3:24).

The next narrative begins with the notice of the birth of Cain and Abel. Cain is a "worker of the ground," ostensibly the result of his father's punishment. After Yahweh rejects Cain's offering of the fruit of the cursed ground, he warns Cain about the temptation of anger. Still, Cain kills his brother Abel and Yahweh confronts him as he did Adam and Eve in Genesis 3. Cain is cursed from the land that he had tilled (Gen 4:11) and is then expelled to somewhere east of Eden (Gen 4:16).

The narrative concludes as it began, with a birth notice. The birth of Cain's son Enoch begins the so-called "Cainite genealogy" (Gen 4:17–22). This list traces six generations of ancestors from Cain to Lamech. In the seventh generation the line segments into three with the sons of Lamech (Jabal, Jubal, and Tubal-Cain), each of whom is credited as the founder of a particular aspect of civilization (tent-dwelling plus cattle-breeding, music, and metallurgy).

As was the case with P's list in Genesis 5, this genealogy also reflects thematic issues present in J's narrative. The list begins with an impulsive murderer, Cain, and concludes with a deliberate and conceited one, Lamech. Evil is transmitted through the generations. As Clines and other have noted, "this has been a progress in sin as much as in civilization."[6]

---

5. See D. L. Peterson, "The Yahwist on the Flood," *VT* 26 (1976) 441.

6. D. J. A. Clines, "Theme in Genesis 1–11," in *I Studied Inscriptions from before the Flood: Ancient Near Eastern, Literary, and Linguistic Approaches to Genesis 1–11* (ed. R. S. Hess and D. T. Tsumura; SBTS 4; Winona Lake, Ind.: Eisenbrauns, 1994) 295; see n. 34; T. Fretheim, *Creation, Fall and Flood* (Minneapolis: Augsburg, 1969) 100.

The "Cainite" genealogy is followed by a second list (Gen 4:25–26), the so-called "Sethite" genealogy, which traces what appears to be a second line from Adam through Seth to Enosh. The current scholarship views these names as the fragmentary remains of a second genealogy in J included alongside the line of Cain.[7] This second list, according to this view, was duplicated in the Priestly genealogy of Gen 5:4–11 and, as a result, was ultimately abridged by the Redactor. The mention of Noah in Gen 5:29, which, as noted earlier, is generally read as a J fragment within P's genealogy, is thought to be a part of this so-called "Sethite genealogy."[8]

The next J episode, Gen 6:1–4, describes the Nephilim, perhaps providing the origins of natural death as opposed to death by murder, perhaps yet another example of the spread of human evil and the motive for the Flood.

The narrative then moves to J's Flood account. In J, the reason for the deluge is made explicit in Gen 6:5–6, "And Yahweh saw that human bad was multiplied in the earth, and every inclination of their heart's thoughts was only bad all the day. And Yahweh regretted that he had made humankind in the earth." In contrast to P, where the entire cosmos became corrupted, here evil is attributed exclusively to humanity. It is an inherent quality increasing and intensifying in direct correspondence to the multiplication of humanity.

Noah, traditionally viewed as the descendant of Seth (the good brother) and Enosh (the first to invoke the name Yahweh), is singled out from his generation and chosen to survive the Flood, though his righteousness is not explicitly noted.[9] After the Flood, Yahweh reacts to Noah's sacrifice by explaining to himself why he will never again curse the ground on account of humankind: "because the inclination of the human heart is bad from their youth" (Gen 8:21). The explanation provided for never cursing the ground again is virtually identical to the original provocation for the Flood itself: compare Gen 6:5, "every inclination of their heart's thoughts was only bad all the day," with Gen 8:21, "the inclination of the human heart is bad from their youth."[10] The Flood does not change human nature.

In the next episode in J, a drunken and naked Noah curses his own son. In other words, humanity's inclination toward evil does not drown with the Flood. Pre-Flood humanity is no different from post-Flood humanity.

---

7. See, for example, C. Westermann, *Genesis 1–11* (trans. J. Scullion; Minneapolis: Augsburg, 1984) 323; and the views cited by J. M. Miller, "The Descendants of Cain: Notes on Genesis 4," *ZAW* 86 (1974) 164.

8. See n. 5. See also the literature cited in Westermann, *Genesis 1–11*, 359.

9. See E. A. Speiser, *Genesis* (AB 1; Garden City, N.Y.: Doubleday, 1985) lxvii, regarding the idiom "find favor," as rarely if ever denoting a moral quality on the part of the designee. See also Peterson, "The Yahwist on the Flood," 441.

10. Ibid.

The apparent inefficacy of the Flood in J compelled Wellhausen to conclude that the whole section of the Deluge, was an "isolated piece" without any connection to the rest of the Yahwist's narrative. This conclusion is at least partially correct; the Flood narrative in all likelihood was adopted and adapted by J from an earlier source.[11] The Flood story may have originated outside of J, but the version as it now stands does convey the language and outlook of the rest of J.[12] Indeed, the discontinuity, so apparent when J is read on its own, need not be the result of the fusion of multiple J "strands." Rather, most of these difficulties arose only when J was inserted beside P in the redacted Torah. Specifically, the placement and present form of the geneaologies of the Primeval History (both J and P) convey a theological purpose that may not have been part of their original design.

P's genealogy in Genesis 5 is apparently a variation of J's "Cainite" genealogy with some minor differences in name placement and spelling. The main difference between the two lists is that P knows nothing of Cain or the murder of Abel but lists Seth as Adam's firstborn and, therefore, most important, son. Humanity is essentially good, created in the image of God. The growth of humanity is a sign of divine blessing. Noah in P is the (firstborn?) son of Lamech, a direct descendant of Adam.

In J, all of humanity, so Gen 4:16–24 implies, descends from Adam through Cain. It is only Gen 4:25–26, the birth of Abel's so-called "replacement," Seth, and his son Enosh, which suggests otherwise. However, Noah's place within these genealogical lists is entirely unclear. Does Gen 5:29, a verse almost unanimously ascribed to J, belong to the Gen 4:25–26 sequence? If so, how is it that this "replacement" line of Seth-Enosh-Noah appears to have no effect on the state of humanity in J's narrative either before (Gen 6:1–4) or after (Gen 9:21ff., 11:1–9) the Flood?

Close examination of Gen 4:25–26 suggests that these verses may not be original to J. The word עוד in 4:25 is uncharacteristic of J. The use of אדם as a proper name as opposed to האדם is particular to P. Similarly, the word אלהים for God in narration is peculiar to P rather than J.[13] The birth of Enosh in Gen 4:26 parallels Gen 5:6 and the sequence Adam-Seth-Enosh agrees with Gen 5:3–8. The only real indicator that both of these verses might belong to J is the notice concerning Enosh at the end of v. 26:

---

11. See the discussion in Westermann, *Genesis 1–11*, 398–405.

12. On J's style, see R. E. Friedman, *Who Wrote the Bible?* (New York: Harper & Row, 1987) 54–69; idem, *The Hidden Book in the Bible* (San Francisco: HarperSanFrancisco, 1998).

13. M. Noth, *A History of Pentateuchal Traditions* (trans. Bernhard W. Anderson; Englewood Cliffs: Prentice-Hall, 1972) 12 n. 26. R. E. Friedman observes that J only uses אלהים in quotation but that the narrator of the story in J refers to the deity exclusively as YHWH. See *The Hidden Book in the Bible*, 353–54. This אלהים is in dialogue.

אז הוחל לקרא בשם יהוה, the assumption that Yahweh was worshiped by his name almost from the beginning of time.[14] However, this portion of the verse could easily be appended to or moved from virtually any other section of the J text. In fact, it follows 4:24 quite naturally—in those violent days people began to pray. I suggest therefore that Gen 4:25–26 are the creation of the Redactor.

Gen 5:29, in contrast, does appear to bear the marks of the Yahwist. The name Yahweh is used in a context where the name Elohim predominates, The etiological etymology of Noah's name, "This one will console us from our labor and from our hands' suffering from the ground which Yahweh has cursed," alludes directly to humanity's need to work the ground, Yahweh's cursing of the soil (Gen 3:17, 18; 4:11), and to Noah's role as the first vintner (Gen 9:20). Such explanations of names do not appear in P. Gen 5:29, therefore, is not part of P's geneaology, nor can it continue to be viewed as part of the so-called "Sethite fragment." Rather, it must somehow be connected to J's genealogy of Cain.

Moreover, Gen 5:28, a verse generally assigned to P, reports that Lamech lived one hundred and eighty-two years and begot 'a son'. The term בן is out of place here. Up to this point in P's list the format has been "and *Personal Name 1* was *X* years old and he begot *Personal Name 2*," presumably citing the name of a firstborn son.[15] Within this genealogy 'son' only appears in the plural form after the name of the firstborn son is mentioned and always in the phrase בנים ובנות. In addition, the only other place in our genealogical lists where the verb ילד appears together with the noun בן is in Gen 4:25–26. If, as we have suggested, Gen 4:25 and 26 are the work of the Redactor, then it is equally plausible that 5:28b is the work of the Redactor, splicing J's account of the birth of Noah into the P list.

J's Song of Lamech (Gen 4:23–24) thus concludes with the birth of his son Noah (in the Toledoth Book, likewise, Noah is the son of Lamech). Read this way in J, Adam, Cain, Lamech, and Noah all have a special relationship to the אדמה. Adam's actions result in Yahweh's curse. Cain's offering, a by-product of this curse, is rejected.[16] Lamech predicts that his son Noah will provide some relief from the labor required to till the cursed ground (Gen 5:29). After the Flood, Yahweh promises to refrain from cursing the ground (or perhaps, not to treat it as cursed), and Noah, the first farmer after the Flood, successfully plants a vineyard. Although it does not cure human evil, J's Flood purifies the state of the ground.

14. Contrast P in Exod 3:14; 6:3.
15. See, for example, Gen 5:6, 9, 12.
16. See G. Herion, "Why God Rejected Cain's Offering: The Obvious Answer," in *Fortunate the Eyes That See: Essays in Honor of David Noel Freedman in Celebration of His*

Why may the Redactor have amended J's text? First, the addition of Gen 4:25–26 smoothed out the tension between the two sources by bringing J into line with P's tradition of Seth as Adam's firstborn (and therefore most important) son.[17] Second, P's Sethite genealogy, placed alongside Noah and the Flood, puts an end to J's line of Cain—victims of the Flood. Rather than all of humanity tracing its origins back to Cain through Lamech and his sons, they now descend from Noah and his three sons, who continue the line of Enosh. This is reiterated in Gen 9:18–19 (also R?), "And Noah's sons who went out from the ark were Shem and Ham and Japhet. And Ham: he was the father of Canaan. *These* three were Noah's sons, and all the earth expanded from *these*."[18]

The Redactor thus uses the genealogies to bring J's primeval history into line with P's. In both P and the redacted Torah, the Flood signifies a new beginning. Subsequently, in P and the redacted Torah, the removal of human evil or sin occurs only through ceremonial atonement and purification.

In J, humanity always possesses the potential to lean toward evil. Sibling rivalry, fratricide, blood vengeance, the ill associated with cities, drunkenness, and illicit sexual relations remain thematic concerns throughout its narrative.[19] Compare, for example, the basic structure of the Flood with J's Sodom-Gomorrah accounts: one righteous man and his family rescued from a corrupt society by God; afterward, his children sexually exploit him while he is inebriated.

Wellhausen sensed the supposed inefficacy of the Yahwist's Flood and chose to remove it from the core of J's narrative, throwing away the baby with the bath water. Perhaps the Redactor of the Torah sought to achieve a similar effect by transplanting Noah from the line of Cain to the line of Seth. It is likely no coincidence that the Flood account is the only major narrative block in the Primeval History in which the Redactor intricately splices together Yahwistic and Priestly traditions.[20] Ultimately, neither the Redactor nor

---

Seventieth Birthday (ed. A. Beck et al.; Grand Rapids: Eerdmans, 1995) 52–65; F. A. Spina, "The 'Ground' for Cain's Rejection (Gen 4): *ᵓᵃdamah* in the Context of Gen 1–11," *ZAW* 104 (1992) 319–32.

17. The Priestly Writer's Sethite genealogy may itself be, as suggested by Westermann and Speiser, a composite list produced by combining the Cainite and Sethite lines reflected in 4:17–18 and 4:25–26.

18. Propp notes a similar technique employed by R in Exodus 6. See W. H. C. Propp, *Exodus 1–18* (AB 2; New York: Doubleday, 1999) 267.

19. See Friedman, Introduction, *The Hidden Book in the Bible*.

20. Peterson, "The Yahwist on the Flood," 438. See also P. J. Harland, *The Value of Human Life: A Study of the Story of the Flood (Gen 6–9)* (VTSup 64; Leiden: Brill, 1996); B. Halpern, "What They Don't Know Won't Hurt Them: Genesis 6–9," in *Fortunate the*

Wellhausen completely succeeded in washing away the Yahwist's true assessment of humanity.

Eyes That See: Essays in Honor of David Noel Freedman in Celebration of His Seventieth Birthday (ed. A. Beck et al.; Grand Rapids: Eerdmans, 1995) 16–34; J. Emerton, "An Examination of Some Attempts to Defend the Unity of the Flood Narrative in Genesis," *VT* 37 (1987) 401–20.

Chapter 5
The Abrahamic Passover

JEFFREY C. GEOGHEGAN

The parallels between Abraham's and Israel's experiences in Egypt are striking.[1]

(1) Both Abraham and Israel *descend* (ירד) to Egypt in search of food during *a heavy famine* (כָבֵד הָרָעָב; Gen 12:10; 43:15; 47:4).

Abraham	Israel
וַיֵּרֶד אַבְרָם מִצְרַיְמָה . . .	וַיֵּרְדוּ [בְּנֵי יִשְׂרָאֵל] מִצְרַיִם . . .
כִּי־כָבֵד הָרָעָב בָּאָרֶץ	כִּי־כָבֵד הָרָעָב בְּאֶרֶץ כְּנַעַן

(2) Both Abraham and Israel are delivered by God through various *plagues* (נֶגַע/נְגָעִים; Gen 12:17a; Exod 11:1a).[2]

Abraham	Israel
וַיְנַגַּע יְהוָה אֶת־פַּרְעֹה	וַיֹּאמֶר יְהוָה אֶל־מֹשֶׁה עוֹד
נְגָעִים גְּדֹלִים וְאֶת־בֵּיתוֹ	נֶגַע אֶחָד אָבִיא עַל־פַּרְעֹה

(3) Both Abraham and Israel (specifically, Moses) are *summoned by Pharaoh* (וַיִּקְרָא פַרְעֹה) prior to their departure (Gen 12:18a; Exod 12:31a).

Author's note: The research presented here was born out of a seminar with Dr. Freedman, and so it seems fitting to include it in a volume honoring the Editor-in-Chief of Biblical Studies on his eightieth birthday. Noel taught (and continues to teach) me more about the Bible and about life than I could have ever hoped to learn in a graduate program in ancient history. My debt to him is enormous, as is my admiration of him.

1. The similarities between Abraham's and Israel's departures from Egypt have been observed by ancient (*Midr. Gen.* 46.6), medieval (Ramban, Nachmanides), and modern (R. Alter, *Genesis* [New York: Norton, 1997] 52; R. E. Friedman, *Commentary on the Torah* [San Francisco: HarperCollins, 2001] 53) commentators.

2. Gen 12:17 and Exod 11:1 mark the first and second occurrences of נֶגַע/נְגָעִים in the Bible.

Abraham	Israel
וַיִּקְרָא פַרְעֹה לְאַבְרָם וַיֹּאמֶר	וַיִּקְרָא פַרְעֹה לְמֹשֶׁה וַיֹּאמֶר

(4) Both Abraham and Israel are *released* (*Piel* of שלח) from Egypt (Gen 12:20; Exod 12:33; cf. Exod 11:1b).

Abraham	Israel
וַתֶּחֱזַק מִצְרַיִם עַל־הָעָם לְמַהֵר לְשַׁלְּחָם וַיְצַו עָלָיו פַּרְעֹה אֲנָשִׁים וַיְשַׁלְּחוּ	
מִן־הָאָרֶץ כִּי אָמְרוּ כֻּלָּנוּ מֵתִים אֹתוֹ וְאֶת־אִשְׁתּוֹ וְאֶת־כָּל־אֲשֶׁר־לוֹ	

(5) Both Abraham and Israel leave Egypt with *great riches* (Gen 13:2; Exod 3:25; 12:35; cf. Gen 12:16, 20).

Abraham	Israel
וְאַבְרָם כָּבֵד מְאֹד בַּמִּקְנֶה בַּכֶּסֶף וּבַזָּהָב	וַיִּשְׁאֲלוּ (בְנֵי־יִשְׂרָאֵל) מִמִּצְרַיִם
	כְּלֵי־כֶסֶף וּכְלֵי זָהָב וּשְׂמָלֹת

Likewise, Jacob's flight from Laban (Genesis 31) is expressed in language that anticipates Israel's flight from Pharaoh.[3]

(1) God *sees* (רָאָה) the *afflictions* (עֳנִי) of both Jacob and Israel (Gen 31:42; Exod 3:7).

Jacob	Israel
אֶת־עָנְיִי וְאֶת־יְגִיעַ כַּפַּי רָאָה אֱלֹהִים	וַיֹּאמֶר יְהוָה רָאֹה רָאִיתִי אֶת־עֳנִי עַמִּי

(2) Both Laban and Pharaoh are *informed* (וַיֻּגַּד) of those *fleeing* (כִּי בָרַח; Gen 31:22; Exod 14:5).

Jacob	Israel
וַיֻּגַּד לְלָבָן בַּיּוֹם הַשְּׁלִישִׁי כִּי בָרַח יַעֲקֹב	וַיֻּגַּד לְמֶלֶךְ מִצְרַיִם כִּי בָרַח הָעָם

(3) Both Laban and Pharaoh *gather* (וַיִּקַּח) reinforcements and *pursue* (וַיִּרְדְּפוּ/וַיִּרְדֹּף) those fleeing (Gen 31:23; Exod 14:7, 9).

Jacob	Israel
וַיִּקַּח אֶת־אֶחָיו עִמּוֹ	וַיִּקַּח שֵׁשׁ־מֵאוֹת רֶכֶב בָּחוּר וְכֹל רֶכֶב
	מִצְרָיִם וְשָׁלִשִׁם עַל־כֻּלּוֹ
וַיִּרְדֹּף אַחֲרָיו	וַיִּרְדְּפוּ מִצְרַיִם אַחֲרֵיהֶם

3. D. Daube, *The Exodus Pattern in the Bible* (London: Faber & Faber, 1963) esp. 62–72; Friedman, *Commentary on the Torah*, 103.

(4) Both Laban and Pharaoh *overtake* (וַיַּשִּׂיגוּ/וַיַּשֵּׂג) the people fleeing near a *mountain* or *hill* (בַּעַל צְפֹן/בְּהַר הַגִּלְעָד;[4] Gen 31:23, 25; Exod 14:9).

Jacob	Israel
וַיַּשֵּׂג לָבָן אֶת־יַעֲקֹב	וַיַּשִּׂיגוּ אוֹתָם . . . לִפְנֵי בַּעַל צְפֹן
וַיַּדְבֵּק אֹתוֹ בְּהַר הַגִּלְעָד	

(5) Both Jacob and Israel do not leave *empty-handed* (רֵיקָם; Gen 31:42; Exod 3:21b).

Jacob	Israel
כִּי עַתָּה רֵיקָם שִׁלַּחְתָּנִי	כִּי תֵלֵכוּן לֹא תֵלְכוּ רֵיקָם

Given the centrality of the exodus for ancient Israel, it is understandable that the biblical authors would want to prefigure this event in the life of Israel's ancestors. After all, to associate the Patriarchs with the exodus would give the nation a profound connection with its past and the Patriarchs an important link with their future—a link that is given explicit expression in God's promise to Abraham concerning his descendants:

וַיֹּאמֶר לְאַבְרָם יָדֹעַ תֵּדַע כִּי־גֵר יִהְיֶה זַרְעֲךָ בְּאֶרֶץ לֹא לָהֶם וַעֲבָדוּם וְעִנּוּ אֹתָם אַרְבַּע מֵאוֹת שָׁנָה: וְגַם אֶת־הַגּוֹי אֲשֶׁר יַעֲבֹדוּ דָּן אָנֹכִי וְאַחֲרֵי־כֵן יֵצְאוּ בִּרְכֻשׁ גָּדוֹל:

And (YHWH) said to Abraham, "Be assured that your offspring will be strangers in a land that is not theirs, and they will be enslaved and oppressed four hundred years; and I will judge the nation they serve, and afterwards they will depart with great riches." (Gen 15:13–14)

In light of this desire to prefigure, even predict, the exodus in the life of the Patriarchs, we should not be surprised to find the central *feast* of the exodus—the Passover, with its Feast of Unleavened Bread—also prefigured in these narratives.[5] I am not referring to the Binding of Isaac (Genesis 22), which at least as early as the book of *Jubilees* was thought to prefigure the paschal ransoming of the firstborn son.[6] I am referring to the destruction of

---

4. This latter connection assumes Baal-Zephon is a mountain; however, its actual location and topographical status are unknown. At Ugarit, it is an epithet for the storm-god Haddu (Baal), whose mountain (Zaphon; present-day Jebel el-Aqraʿ) is located about 40 km north of Ras Shamra. Several sites have been proposed for the Egyptian Baal-Zephon, most notably Mt. Casios near Lake Sirbonis. Yet whether the biblical writers understood Baal-Zephon to be a mountain is unclear.

5. On the relationship between the Passover and the Feast of Unleavened Bread, see W. H. C. Propp, *Exodus 1–18: A New Translation with Introduction and Commentary* (AB 2; New York: Doubleday, 1999) 428–44.

6. *Jub.* 17:15–16; cf. also *Mek. Pishā* 7; *Exod. Rab.* 15:11.

Sodom and Gomorrah (Genesis 18 and 19), where Abraham and Lot partake of a meal with their divine visitors just prior to those cities' demise. As in the examples above, a number of the narrative details in the Sodom and Gomorrah story find parallels in the account of the Passover. It is the purpose of this essay to explore these parallels in order to determine if Genesis 18 and 19 were, in fact, intended to prefigure the Passover. The ramifications of our findings on the composition of the biblical narratives will be considered at the conclusion of our study.

God _Descends_ Because of a _Cry_ That _Ascends_ to Him

At the Burning Bush, YHWH informs Moses that "the cry of the sons of Israel" has "come to [him]," that he has "seen" and "knows" of their suffering, and that he has "come down" to deliver them (Exod 3:7–9). The parallels with God's visit to Abraham are noteworthy:

וַיֹּאמֶר יְהוָה זַעֲקַת סְדֹם וַעֲמֹרָה כִּי־רָבָּה וְחַטָּאתָם כִּי כָבְדָה מְאֹד׃
אֵרֲדָה־נָּא וְאֶרְאֶה הַכְּצַעֲקָתָהּ הַבָּאָה אֵלַי עָשׂוּ כָּלָה וְאִם־לֹא אֵדָעָה׃

And YHWH said, "_The cry of Sodom and Gomorrah_ is great and their sin is exceedingly onerous. Let me _descend_ and _see_ if they have acted according to the _cry that has come to me_; and if not, let me _know._" (Gen 18:20–21)

These parallels go beyond mere thematic similarities but reflect specific linguistic equivalencies, as the following table demonstrates.

Sodom Narrative Genesis 18:20–21	*Exodus Narrative* Exodus 3:7–9
זַעֲקַת סְדֹם וַעֲמֹרָה⁷ הַבָּאָה אֵלַי אֵרֲדָה וְאֶרְאֶה אֵדָעָה	צַעֲקַת בְּנֵי־יִשְׂרָאֵל בָּאָה אֵלַי וָאֵרֵד רָאִיתִי יָדַעְתִּי

Nowhere in the Hebrew Bible do we find all of these activities mentioned together, let alone in reference to God.

It is possible, however, that these parallels are the result of some other factor. For example, one might expect to find shared vocabulary in narratives recounting similar events (i.e., divine visitations prior to judgment or deliverance). Thus, in the Tower of Babel narrative, God "descends" to "see" the

---

7. While the variant spelling of זַעֲקַת/צַעֲקַת might seem to weaken the above parallels, the next verse (Gen 18:21) has צַעֲקָה (הַכְּצַעֲקָתָהּ), and there is textual evidence (Samaritan) for צַעֲקַת in Gen 18:20. See also the discussion of צעקתם (Gen 19:13; Exod 3:7), below.

tower before rendering judgment (Gen 11:5), and, when Israel is being oppressed by the Philistines, God announces that he "has seen" their suffering and that "their cry has come to [him]" (1 Sam 9:16). Still, it is the number of parallels between the Sodom and Gomorrah and the Burning Bush accounts (several more than in these other examples) that suggests there is more going on than just the conventions of storytelling.

Further suggesting that these parallels are purposeful is that they help to explain an enigmatic statement made by Lot's guests. In Gen 19:13, the angels inform Lot that YHWH intends to destroy Sodom because of 'their cry' (צעקתם). This remark is ambiguous. Whose cry? The matter is further complicated by the earlier reference to the "cry of Sodom and Gomorrah" in Gen 18:20. Whose cry within Sodom and Gomorrah? The righteous who dwell there? Presumably there are none righteous except Lot and his family (and even their righteousness is suspect). If "their cry" refers to Lot's and his family's, then why would the angels say "their" when speaking to Lot? They should say "your."

Rabbinic commentators, aware of these difficulties, suggested that "their cry" referred to the cries of travelers who had been assaulted by the inhabitants of Sodom and Gomorrah but who had since moved on. This allowed for the cries to derive from someone other than Lot and his family (thus explaining the use of "their"), as well as from people no longer residing in Sodom and Gomorrah (because God would not destroy the righteous with the wicked; Gen 18:23–26). According to these commentators, even Abraham's servant, Eliezer, fell victim to Sodom's abuses while visiting Lot.[8] Although these explanations make for interesting midrash, there is little in the text to recommend them.

Another possible explanation is that "their cry" refers to Sodom's and Gomorrah's immorality. Thus, the JPSV renders this phrase "their *outrage.*" While this understanding helps to smooth out the difficulties caused by the presence of צעקתם in Genesis 19, it is contrary to every other use of צעקה in the Torah,[9] including by this same author.[10] There is, however, another solution, one that *is* supported by the text and that allows us to render צעקה according to its usual sense.

---

8. For the rabbinic traditions surrounding Sodom's wickedness, including its effect on Lot, Eliezer, and others, see *HaYashar,* Wa-Yera, 35b–38a.

9. Compare Exod 11:6; 12:30; and 22:23, where צעקה refers to the "cry" of those wronged and not to the wrongs themselves. One possible exception, although outside the Torah, is Isa 5:7, where God searches for righteousness, and finds "a cry."

10. "Their cry" in both Gen 19:13 and Exod 3:7 would seem to belong to J, and in the latter case these words refer to the anguish of those suffering, not to the Egyptians' acts of oppression. See also Gen 27:34 (J).

"Their cry" (צעקתם) appears only one other time in the Hebrew Bible, in the very passage yielding our other parallels—the Burning Bush narrative:

וַיֹּאמֶר יְהוָה רָאֹה רָאִיתִי אֶת־עֳנִי עַמִּי אֲשֶׁר בְּמִצְרָיִם וְאֶת־צַעֲקָתָם שָׁמַעְתִּי מִפְּנֵי נֹגְשָׂיו
כִּי יָדַעְתִּי אֶת־מַכְאֹבָיו

And YHWH said, "I have most certainly seen the oppression of my people who are in Egypt, and I have heard *their cry* in the presence of their taskmasters, for I know their sufferings." (Exod 3:7)

Here "their cry" makes sense: it refers to Israel's cries due to their Egyptian bondage. The fact that in Genesis 19 "their cry" does not make (immediate) sense suggests that its presence there serves another purpose: namely, to provide another linguistic parallel between the Sodom and Gomorrrah narrative and the events of the exodus. Yet, in this particular case the awkwardness introduced by the presence of "their cry" into the Sodom and Gomorrah account serves the added purpose of making these connections more obvious.

Abraham/Israel Partake of Meals That Include Cakes (עגות) and Unleavened Bread (מצות)

The parallels between the Sodom and Gomorrah and the Passover narratives are also reflected in the menu items offered by Abraham and Lot to their divine guests. Specifically, when the three visitors arrive at Abraham's camp, Abraham asks Sarah to make 'cakes' עגות (Gen 18:6). Then, when the two angels continue on to Sodom, Lot serves them 'unleavened bread' מצות (Gen 19:3). The choice of these two particular food items is significant, for, although the term מצות is found frequently in the biblical text, it first appears here, and then it is not found again *until the Passover*, where it plays a central role in that narrative (Exod 12:8, 15, 17, 18, 20, 39; 13:6, 7). Similarly, the word עגות first appears in the Sodom and Gomorrah narrative, and then it is not seen again *until the Passover*, where it is used together with מצות (Exod 12:39).

The presence of מצות in the Sodom and Gomorrah narrative takes on added significance when we consider that unleavened bread is usually reserved for the Feast of Unleavened Bread and other cultic (or priestly) meals.[11] Therefore, its presence in this narrative is unusual and seems to

---

11. One exception is Saul's consumption of the unleavened bread prepared by the medium of Endor (1 Sam 28:24). This episode, however, may be the exception that proves the rule. Saul's partaking of food reserved for priests (and with a medium, no less) seems intended as a further slur on his character and provides a stark contrast to Abraham's (and Lot's) meals with their divine guests. This contrast would be all the more striking if these narratives were originally part of a shorter work (namely, the J source; see R. E. Friedman, *The Hidden Book in the Bible* [San Francisco: HarperCollins, 1998] 81–86 and 228–30).

convey the sacred nature of Lot's meal. Supporting this conclusion is the fact that in the companion narrative to Genesis 19—the sin at Gibeah in Judges 19—many of the details are the same, with at least one notable exception: the unleavened bread has been removed (Judg 19:19, 21).[12] If the meal shared by Lot and his guests was thought to have cultic or sacred significance, perhaps even to prefigure the Passover, then the choice to change the dinner items in Judges 19 would be understandable, even expected.

The significance of these menu items did not escape the attention of later exegetes. Rashi, for example, when commenting on the presence of unleavened bread in Genesis 19, simply states: "It was the Passover" (היה פסח).[13]

The Meal of עגות and מצות Occurs at an Appointed Time

Another indication that the Sodom and Gomorrah account was intended to point forward to the Passover is found in the announcement of Isaac's birth. In Gen 18:14, YHWH promises Abraham that he will have a son 'at the appointed time' (למועד). Although מועד is used numerous times in the Torah (particularly for the 'Tent of Meeting' אהל מועד[14]), למועד (with the prepositional ל) only occurs in connection with two events: (1) Isaac's birth and (2) the Feast of Unleavened Bread.[15] While this may be merely fortuitous, it seems significant that three different passages, representing at least

---

Compare 1 Sam 13:8–14, where Saul similarly oversteps his prerogatives as king by offering a sacrifice.

12. The parallels between Genesis 19 and Judges 19 are patent. For a recent treatment of these similarities, see Friedman (*The Hidden Book in the Bible*, 18–19).

13. Although it may be coincidence, it is worth observing that the angels turn aside into Lot's house to eat their meal of unleavened bread 'in the evening' (בָּעֶרֶב), the same time designated for the eating of unleavened bread during the Passover (Exod 12:18):

In the first (month), on the fourteenth day of the month, *in the evening*, you will eat unleavened bread, until the twenty-first day of the month, *in the evening*.

בָּרִאשֹׁן בְּאַרְבָּעָה עָשָׂר יוֹם לַחֹדֶשׁ בָּעֶרֶב תֹּאכְלוּ מַצֹּת עַד יוֹם הָאֶחָד וְעֶשְׂרִים
לַחֹדֶשׁ בָּעָרֶב:

14. Exod 27:21; 28:43; 29:4, 10, 11, 30, 32, 42, 44; 30:16, 18, etc.

15. Isaac's birth: Gen 17:21; 18:14; 21:2; The Passover: Exod 13:10; 23:15; 34:18. The distinction between לַמּוֹעֵד and לְמוֹעֵד is due to the latter's being in construct (with 'its' [לְמוֹעֲדָהּ; Exod 13:10] and 'the month of Abib' [לְמוֹעֵד חֹדֶשׁ הָאָבִיב]; Exod 23:15; 34:18], respectively) and does not affect the observation that these are the only examples of מועד with the prepositional ל in the Torah (although, see the plural למועדים in Gen 1:14). As an additional observation, למועד in Exod 23:15 and 34:18 could be vocalized לְמוֹעֵד חֹדֶשׁ הָאָבִיב ('at the appointed time of the month of Abib' [with the Masoretes]) or לַמּוֹעֵד חֹדֶשׁ הָאָבִיב ('at the appointed time, the month of Abib').

two different sources,[16] record that Isaac's birth was to occur "at the appointed time." This would suggest that למועד was an important part of the traditions surrounding Isaac's birth.[17] When we consider that למועד similarly appears three times in connection with the Feast of Unleavened Bread, and again in contexts representing at least two different sources,[18] then it would seem that this phrase also had strong associations with the Passover. That is, someone hearing that Isaac's birth occurred למועד could understandably make the connection with the only other event in the Torah occurring למועד: the Passover.[19] Ramban, in fact, seems to have made such a connection. When commenting on the use of למועד in Gen 17:21, he writes:

16. At minimum, למועד is used by P (Gen 17:21) and J (Gen 18:14). Source designations are more difficult in Gen 21:2. It appears that the Redactor (R) has interwoven both J and P in Gen 21:1–2. Thus, למועד in v. 2 may derive from J, P, or even R (under the influence of J and/or P).

17. Whether the use of למועד in connection with Isaac's birth was solidified at an oral or written stage of the tradition is not important for our purposes. What *is* important is that למועד was significant enough to be repeated three times, and by more than one source, in connection with this event.

18. Exod 13:10 (E, R, or possibly D; see Propp, *Exodus*, 373–78); Exod 23:15 (Covenant Code [an independent source] or E); and Exod 34:18 (J).

19. There may even be an indication that the meals eaten by Abraham and Lot with their divine guests occurred at the time appointed for the Passover: the spring. The evidence, though admittedly tenuous (since it hinges on the translation of one phrase), is this: in the Passover formulas we read that the Feast of Unleavened Bread was to be observed 'at the appointed time of the month of Abib' למועד חודש האביב (Exod 23:15; 34:18). The time of Isaac's birth, as mentioned above, is also למועד, which is further specified by the phrase כעת חיה. The question is: What does this phrase mean? The general consensus is that כעת חיה means 'this time next year' (see, for example, O. Loretz, "*Kᶜt ḥyh*—'wie jetzt ums Jahr': Gen 18:10," *Bib* 43 [1962] 75–78; R. Yaron, "KAᶜETH ḤAYYAH AND KOH LEḤAY," *VT* 12 [1962] 500–501; M. Cogan and H. Tadmor, *II Kings* [AB 11; Garden City, N.Y.: Doubleday, 1988] 57 n. 16; M. I. Gruber, "The Reality behind the Hebrew Expression כעת חיה," *ZAW* 103 [1991] 271–74), an understanding that is thought to be confirmed by P's use of בשנה האחרת in his version of the promise of Isaac's birth (Gen 17:21). By this account, בשנה האחרת is P's translation of J's more arcane כעת חיה (Gen 18:10, 14). Yet this suggestion is itself important if P is providing a "translation" of a phrase that had fallen out of use or the meaning of which may no longer have been known. The phrase might literally be rendered "the time of living" or "the time of reviving," which some have understood to mean the spring. Brown, Driver, and Briggs (312b) propose this interpretation, and certain translations render it thus. The RSV translates Gen 18:14b: "At the appointed time I will return to you, in the spring, and Sarah shall have a son." One could imagine a scenario where כעת חיה originally meant 'spring', but, because the spring also marked the beginning of a new year, it came to denote 'next year'. If the author of Genesis 18 (J) wanted to specify the spring using an alternative to האביב, then כעת חיה may have suited his purposes. In an analogous situation, Jacob's flight from Laban (with its several parallels to the exodus) is set in the spring, but the author has let his audience know this

The scripture says "at the appointed time in the following year": this refers to what follows in *Wa-Yera*, because the announcement (of Isaac's birth) was during Passover, and during the following Passover Isaac was born.

Similarly, *Midr. Tanḥuma* says concerning the announcement of Isaac's birth:

Sarah was visited at the beginning of the year, and Isaac was born a year later, on the night of Passover.

Initial Observations

The parallels outlined above seem significant enough to make the case for the prefiguring of the Passover in the life of Abraham. Nowhere else do we encounter these exact linguistic and thematic parallels. Yet there are other parallels that, though less compelling, are worth mentioning for what they contribute to the overall sense that Abraham and Lot are participating in a paschal-like event.

God *Passes Over* Abraham/Israel in Order to Destroy a Rebellious People

As the three visitors approach Abraham's camp, the nature of their movement is described:

וַיֹּאמַר אֲדֹנָי אִם־נָא מָצָאתִי חֵן בְּעֵינֶיךָ אַל־נָא תַעֲבֹר מֵעַל עַבְדֶּךָ: וְאֶקְחָה פַת־לֶחֶם
וְסַעֲדוּ לִבְּכֶם אַחַר תַּעֲבֹרוּ כִּי־עַל־כֵּן עֲבַרְתֶּם עַל־עַבְדְּכֶם

And Abraham said, "My Lord, if I have found favor in your eyes, do not *pass by* your servant. . . . Let me get a little bread, and you can refresh yourselves, and afterward you may *pass by*, since you are *passing by* your servant. (Gen 18:3, 5a)

The repetition of עבר is peculiar, especially when we consider that it has only occurred three times in Genesis thus far.[20] Here it appears three times in two verses. Significantly, the next time עבר is used to describe YHWH's movements is *during the Passover*, when he "passes through" Egypt. In fact, in both of its appearances in Exodus 12, עבר is used in connection with (perhaps even in parallelism with) פסח, the "technical" term for God's activity during the Passover.[21] In Exod 12:12–13, for example, YHWH tells Moses,

---

subtly, with the notice that Laban and his sons were shearing their sheep. On shearing as a springtime activity in ancient Israel, see S. Hirsch, *Sheep and Goats in Palestine* (Tel Aviv: Palestine Economic Society [Omanuth Erez-Israel], 1933) 29. For the reasons why an author might choose to be subtle in foreshadowing the Passover, see the discussion below.

20. Gen 8:1; 12:6; and 15:17.

21. On the possibility that פסח and עבר are being used in parallelism, see Propp, *Exodus*, 401.

וְעָבַרְתִּי בְאֶרֶץ־מִצְרַיִם בַּלַּיְלָה הַזֶּה וְהִכֵּיתִי כָל־בְּכוֹר בְּאֶרֶץ מִצְרַיִם וּפָסַחְתִּי עֲלֵכֶם
וְלֹא־יִהְיֶה בָכֶם נֶגֶף לְמַשְׁחִית בְּהַכֹּתִי בְּאֶרֶץ מִצְרַיִם

And I will *pass through* (עבר) the land of Egypt this night, and I will strike down all the firstborn in the land of Egypt . . . and I will *pass over/protect*[22] (פסח) you, and there will not be a destructive blow against you when I strike down the land of Egypt.

And again, in Exod 12:23, Moses informs the elders,

וְעָבַר יְהוָה לִנְגֹּף אֶת־מִצְרַיִם וְרָאָה אֶת־הַדָּם עַל־הַמַּשְׁקוֹף וְעַל שְׁתֵּי הַמְּזוּזֹת וּפָסַח
יְהוָה עַל־הַפֶּתַח וְלֹא יִתֵּן הַמַּשְׁחִית לָבֹא אֶל־בָּתֵּיכֶם לִנְגֹּף:

When Yhwh *passes through* (עבר) in order to strike the Egyptians, he will see the blood on the lintel and upon the two doorposts and Yhwh will *pass over/protect* (פסח) the entrance and he will not allow the Destroyer to enter into your houses in order to strike.

Again, the fact that these mark the first and second passages in which God 'passes by' (עבר) something in the biblical text seems significant.[23]

Also noteworthy is the reference in the Sodom and Gomorrah narrative to God's and the angels' activity of 'destroying' (מַשְׁחִתִים/מַשְׁחִית; Gen 19:13, 14).[24] As with the example just cited (and a number of the other

---

22. On the variety of possible meanings for פסח, including 'to pass over', 'to protect', 'to limp', 'to skip', and 'to dance', see Propp, *Exodus*, 398–99, 401. I prefer 'to pass over', seeing פסח and עבר in parallelism in Exod 12:13 and 23, the difference being what is done when God passes over Egypt and Israel ('to strike' versus 'not to allow the destroyer to enter your houses to strike' [v. 23]). Friedman's 'to halt at' provides another possible solution to the difficulties in rendering פסח (*Commentary on the Torah*, 207, 209).

23. If "the furnace of smoke" and "flame of fire" that pass between the animal halves during Abraham's covenant ceremony are, in fact, a theophany of Yhwh (Gen 15:17), then Gen 18:3 and 5 and Exod 12:12–13 and 23 mark the second and third occurrences of God's 'passing by/through'. This observation may itself be important if the theophany of a smoking furnace and a flaming fire foreshadows the theophany of the pillar of cloud (smoke?) and fire of the exodus and wilderness wanderings (see, for example, Exod 13:21; Num 14:14).

24. While confusion between divine and angelic activity and speech occurs elsewhere in the biblical text (see, for example, Gen 22:10–18; 32:25–31; Judg 6:11–24), in Genesis 19 it appears that both the angels and God are active in the destruction of Sodom and Gomorrah. The evidence for this is that the angels make a distinction between their activity and God's ("Yhwh has sent *us* to destroy it" [Gen 19:13]), yet God is also said to participate in the destruction ("Yhwh rained brimstone and fire upon Sodom and Gomorrah" [Gen 19:24]). Similarly, in the exodus account, both God and "the Destroyer" seem to play their separate parts (Exod 12:12–13, 23). See also n. 25. It is possible, however, that in both accounts angels are the medium (immediate cause) through which God renders judgment (ultimate cause). Another possibility is that angels are a concrete representation (hypostasis) of God, upon whom humans are otherwise unable to look and live (Exod 33:20). For this

parallels already mentioned), the next occurrence of מַשְׁחִית is *during the Passover*, where it is used both for the 'destructive blow' (נֶגֶף לְמַשְׁחִית; presumably Yahweh's[25]) and 'the Destroyer' (הַמַּשְׁחִית; presumably an angelic- or demonic-being[26]), who seeks to kill the firstborn of Egypt.[27] Thus, it might be said that in both narratives, God, accompanied by his "destroying" angel(s), *passes by* his elect on his way to render judgment upon a rebellious people.[28]

Abraham/Israel Hurries

Similar to עבר, the verbal root מהר ('to hurry') is repeated three times in the span of two verses (Gen 18:6–7). Abraham 'hurries' (וימהר) to Sarah, where he instructs her to 'hurriedly' (מהרי) make 'cakes' (עגות). He then 'runs' (רץ) to his servant, who 'hurriedly' (וימהר) prepares a calf.

Hurrying may simply be what one does when God (or anyone unexpected) shows up for dinner. However, hurrying also plays an important role in the Passover. In Exod 12:11, for example, the Israelites are told to eat the paschal meal 'in haste' (בחפזון).[29] Then, in Exod 12:33, with language more closely tied to the Abrahamic narrative, the Egyptians are described as being 'strong' (ותחזק) upon the Israelites 'to hurry to release' (למהר לשלחם). Later we read that due to the Egyptians' intervention the Israelites were 'unable to tarry' (ולא יכלו להתמהמה; Exod 12:39).

The similarities with Lot's flight from Sodom are interesting. Despite the angel's instructions to flee Sodom immediately, the text records that Lot 'tarried' (ויתמהמה; Gen 19:16). As a result, the angels 'seize' (ויחזקו) Lot and his

---

view, see R. E. Friedman, *The Hidden Face of God* (San Francisco: HarperCollins, 1995) 10–11; and *Commentary on the Torah*, 63.

25. YHWH's words 'in my striking the land of Egypt' (בְּהַכֹּתִי בְּאֶרֶץ מִצְרָיִם), which immediately follow נֶגֶף לְמַשְׁחִית, suggest that this is YHWH's 'destructive blow'. Conceivably, however, נֶגֶף לְמַשְׁחִית could be rendered 'the blow from the Destroyer' and, conversely, וְלֹא יִתֵּן הַמַּשְׁחִית could be rendered 'and [YHWH] will not allow destruction'. See Propp, *Exodus*, 401–2.

26. Compare the "destroying angel/messenger" of 2 Sam 24:16 and 1 Chr 21:12, 15. For the possibility that 'the Destroyer' (המשחית) is a demonic figure, see Propp, *Exodus*, 401.

27. Interestingly, Ps 78:49 describes the destruction of the firstborn of Egypt as occurring by the agency of more than one angel, perhaps an example in which the events surrounding the destruction of Sodom and Gomorrah have influenced the retelling of the Passover (see the comments on Jer 31:32a, below, for another possible example of this).

28. Admittedly, the parallels are not exact, because God does not *pass by* Abraham but stops and eats a meal with him. Yet, it may be in this difference that Abraham stands out as the paschal participant par excellence, since the deity and his destroying angels both pass by Abraham *and* join him in his observance of the Passover meal.

29. Hebrew בחפזון is a rare word, only appearing two other times in the Hebrew Bible: once as a reminder of the Passover event (Deut 16:3), and again in imagery borrowed from this event to illustrate Israel's redemption from exile (Isa 52:12).

family by the hands and lead them out of the city. In light of these parallels, it is interesting that the author of Jer 31:32, when reminding Israel of the way that God delivered them from Egypt, uses language more descriptive of Lot's rescue from Sodom than any used to describe Israel's redemption from Egypt:

לֹא כַבְּרִית אֲשֶׁר כָּרַתִּי אֶת־אֲבוֹתָם בְּיוֹם הֶחֱזִיקִי בְיָדָם לְהוֹצִיאָם מֵאֶרֶץ מִצְרָיִם

[The covenant I will make] will not be like the covenant I made with their fathers in *the day I seized them by the hand to lead them out of the land of Egypt.* (Jer 31:32a)

Whether or not the author of this passage was influenced by the Sodom and Gomorrah narrative when recounting the events of the exodus we cannot say. However, the possibility that the imagery of Lot's escape from Sodom would evoke such comparisons is certainly understandable when we consider the number of other parallels between these two narratives.

The Command to <u>*Rise Up and Go from*</u> *the Place of Destruction*

As the last plague is taking its toll on the Egyptians, Pharaoh summons Moses and Aaron and says, "Get up and go out from the midst of my people" (Exod 12:31). These exact words, 'Get up and go from . . .' (וַיֹּאמֶר קוּמוּ צְאוּ מִן), are found only one other time in the Hebrew Bible—the Sodom and Gomorrah narrative, when Lot warns his sons-in-law to leave the city:

וַיֹּאמֶר קוּמוּ צְּאוּ מִן־הַמָּקוֹם הַזֶּה כִּי־מַשְׁחִית יְהוָה אֶת־הָעִיר

And he said, "Get up and go out from this place because YHWH is destroying the city." (Gen 19:14)

An obvious difference between these narratives is that Moses and Aaron heed this command while Lot's sons-in-law do not. However, the presence of the same command in both episodes further establishes the connection between these narratives.

As a final note: just as the time of Lot's meal of מצות corresponds to the time designated for the eating of מצות during Passover (בערב; cf. Gen 19:1 and Exod 12:18), so the command to arise and flee from the place of destruction is given at the same time that it is given during the Passover (ה[לילה]; cf. Gen 19:5, 14–15 and Exod 12:30–31).

Summary

The parallels outlined above were striking enough for the midrash and rabbinic commentators to associate the events surrounding the destruction of

Sodom and Gomorrah with the Passover. And I would suspect that an Israelite audience, when hearing specific turns of phrases and references to items known also (and, in many cases, *only*) from the Passover, would have made similar associations—especially if they had already been "primed" for such paschal imagery by the earlier allusions to the exodus in the life of Abraham (Genesis 12 and 15).

If the Passover *is* prefigured in the Sodom and Gomorrah narrative, then within the life of Abraham we find the sojourn to and exodus from Egypt (Genesis 12), a prediction of the exodus (Genesis 15), the Passover with its Feast of Unleavened Bread (Genesis 18 and 19) and, perhaps, the Ransom of the Firstborn (Genesis 22),[30] demonstrating that Abraham truly was the father of the nation. In the words of Ramban:

כל מה שאירע לאבות סימן לבנים

Everything that happens to the Patriarchs is a pattern for the children.

Concluding Matters

If the above observations are correct about the Passover's being prefigured in the Sodom and Gomorrah narrative, then we are left with at least two questions: (1) who is responsible for these paschal allusions, and (2) why did those responsible not make these allusions more explicit?

Regarding who is responsible: We can trace the parallels describing God's visits to Abraham (Gen 18:20–21) and Moses (Exod 3:7–8) to a single source (J). This would suggest that this same source is responsible for the other parallels observed in Exodus 12. However, recent studies have suggested that there is little if any J in the Passover narrative.[31] If these studies prove correct, this does not necessarily undermine the argument for paschal allusions in J's Sodom and Gomorrah account, just as it does not invalidate the presence of other allusions to the exodus in J (Gen 12:10–20); nor does the absence of J in the Passover mean that an editor consciously inserted J-like language into Exodus 12 in order to produce these parallels, since much of the paschal imagery found in the Sodom and Gomorrah account ("unleavened bread," "hurrying," "destroying," and so on) would likely have existed in anyone's account of the Passover. That J *did* have an account of the Passover, however,

---

30. Several parallels exist between the ransoming of the firstborn in the Akedah and Passover: (1) the endangerment of a firstborn son, (2) the connection *within the story* between the mountain of Isaac's binding and sacrifice at the Temple (Gen 22:14b; cf. 2 Chr 3:1), the location of the later Passover sacrifice (Deut 16:2, 6; 2 Kgs 23:23; 2 Chr 30:1), and (3) the substitutionary death of an ovine (Gen 22:13; Exod 13:15).

31. See Propp (*Exodus*, esp. pp. 373–80) for a recent treatment of sources in Exodus 12.

is strongly suggested by J's allusion to this event in the Abrahamic narratives
(Gen 12:10–20) and J's inclusion of the Passover in his Ten Commandments (Exod 34:18).[32] Moreover, there is evidence that an editor *was* aware
of, and may have even contributed to, J's attempts to prefigure the Passover
in the life of Abraham, even if that editor did not incorporate J's Passover account into Exodus 12.

First, the prediction of Israel's future bondage and eventual release from
Egypt (Gen 15:13–16) shows signs of redactional activity and may even derive from the Redactor himself. Several pieces of evidence suggest this: (1) the
use of *Wiederaufnahme* (resumptive repetition) in vv. 12 and 17, which often
(though not always) points to inserted material, (2) the presence of data and
terminology characteristic of J, E, and P individually, and (3) the seeming
contradiction between v. 5, where Abraham is directed to look at the stars,
and v. 12, where the sun is beginning to set (and continues to set as late as
v. 17).[33] If Gen 15:13–16 is from the Redactor (R, given the presence of J, E,
and P terminology), then this would suggest that he was aware of the exodus
imagery in the life of Abraham from his sources (Gen 12:10–20) and that he
even sought to make his own contribution.[34] As Friedman observes, the prediction of the exodus in the life of Abraham would "enhance the connection
between the patriarchal stories of Genesis and the slavery-exodus story in Exodus and . . . enhance the union of the sources themselves"—worthy aims for
an editor attempting to unite diverse sources into a coherent narrative.

Another piece of evidence that suggests the Redactor (R) was alert to the
exodus imagery in the life of Abraham in general, and to the paschal imagery
in Genesis 18 and 19 in particular, is the way in which he brought his sources
together. At the end of Genesis 17 (P), for example, God commands Abraham to be circumcised as a sign of the covenant—a command that Abraham
and his household fulfilled "that very day":

> And Abraham and his son Ishmael were circumcised on that very day; and all
> the men of his house, those born in his house and those purchased from
> strangers, were circumcised with him. (Gen 17:26–27)

---

32. It may even be that, in J's account of the Passover, the parallels with the Sodom
and Gomorrah narrative were more apparent (see below).

33. Friedman, *Who Wrote the Bible?* 256.

34. D. N. Freedman, M. Homan, and I (*The Nine Commandments: Uncovering the
Hidden Pattern of Crime and Punishment in the Hebrew Bible* [New York: Doubleday,
2000]) have made a similar argument to explain how a pattern of command violations
spanning from Exodus to 2 Kings could exist in a corpus that includes several different
stages of biblical composition and compilation. In that case our solution is, simply put, that
much of the pattern was already present but that an alert editor arranged and, in some cases,
inserted (see especially Lev 24:10–16 and Num 15:32–36) material to bring that pattern
into sharper relief.

This same language concerning circumcision is found in *only one other place in the Hebrew Bible*—during the exodus (Exod 12:43–49), when God gives Moses the requirements for participation in the Passover:

> This is the law of the Passover . . . any slave bought with money must be circumcised; then he may eat of it. . . . And if a sojourner dwells with you and desires to observe the Passover to YHWH, all his males must be circumcised, and then he may approach to observe it, and he will be like a native of the land. But no uncircumcised person may eat of it. (Exod 12:48)

Abraham's circumcision in Genesis 17 immediately prior to his paschal-like meal in Genesis 18 may be coincidence. Perhaps the command to circumcise one's male offspring fits most naturally after the promise to Abraham that he would bear a son, and, therefore, the editor was unaware of the effect he was creating. Yet its placement prior to Abraham's meal is certainly fortuitous and may be purposeful, even if convenient for narrative and logical considerations. That is, the redactor, aware of the paschal implications of Abraham's meal in Genesis 18, felt Abraham should be circumcised in obedience to the paschal laws expressed in Exodus 12.[35] Propp observes:

> There is a curious association between Pesaḥ and circumcision. In Gen 17:12, P requires that all males be circumcised on the eighth day. When P next mentions circumcision (excluding Moses' "uncircumcised" lips [6:12, 30]), it is as a precondition for participation in the Pesaḥ (12:44, 48).[36]

Propp's observation fits the pattern noted above: something mentioned first in connection with the Sodom and Gomorrah narrative does not appear again until the Passover (compare, for example, עגות and מצות).

This leaves us with the question of why the paschal allusions in Genesis 18 and 19 were not made more explicit. This is a difficult question to answer, because it requires an understanding of the methods and motives of those involved (both as authors and editors) in producing the biblical text as we have it. However, the following are some suggestions.

Perhaps the combining of sources obscured what were originally clearer allusions. For example, with the exclusion of J's account of the Passover in Exodus 12, maybe the more explicit parallels between this narrative and the Sodom and Gomorrah pericope were lost.[37] Importantly, Propp makes a similar case for the "bridegroom of blood" pericope (Exod 4:24–25), arguing

---

35. See Josh 5:2–9 for another example of circumcision prior to participation in the Passover.

36. Propp, *Exodus*, 452.

37. See the presence of very specific linguistic parallels between J's Sodom and Gomorrah narrative and the J material in the Burning Bush account (discussed above).

that the paschal allusions present in this narrative may have been more apparent had J's Passover account been preserved.[38]

Perhaps the paschal allusions in the Sodom and Gomorrah narrative seem subtle to us, but to an Israelite audience they would have been more obvious. As noted above, the presence of similar terms and phrases likely would have produced such associations in the minds of those intimately acquainted with these traditions. Instructive here may be the ability of the rabbinic commentators to perceive connections in the text that modern exegetes often miss— including the present case of paschal allusions in Abraham's and Lot's meals.[39]

Finally, perhaps those responsible for the paschal allusions in the patriarchal narratives desired to be subtle, skillfully weaving portents of later events into earlier narratives, leaving their discovery to others.[40] Dr. Freedman has made a similar argument for the Primary History, noting that the references to Babel (Gen 11:9) and the Chaldeans (Gen 11:28, 31) near the beginning of this work point forward to Israel's eventual Babylonian exile at the hands of the Chaldeans at the end of this work (2 Kings 24–25).

Whatever the full reasons for this subtlety, the result has been a literary masterpiece whose many treasures may still remain hidden—leaving you, Noel, with plenty still to do.

---

38. Propp, *Exodus*, 238.

39. Admittedly, these same commentators "perceive" things in the text that are sometimes quite suspect. Yet maybe the biblical authors counted on a similar creativity in their audience. Consider, for example, many of the wordplays in the biblical text (e.g., *bālal* versus "Babel" in Gen 11:9), which require a certain amount of "free association."

40. D. N. Freedman, *The Unity of the Hebrew Bible* (Ann Arbor: University of Michigan Press, 1991) 9. Compare also the so-called "rape of Dinah" (Genesis 34), which seems to anticipate the rape of Tamar (2 Samuel 13). Such foreshadowing is seldom made explicit by the biblical authors.

Chapter 6

Archaeology and the Shasu Nomads: Recent Excavations in the Jabal Hamrat Fidan, Jordan

THOMAS E. LEVY, RUSSELL B. ADAMS, AND ADOLFO MUNIZ

Introduction

Biblical scholars view the Late Bronze Age and Early Iron as the period during which the tribes of Israel settled in Canaan, as described at length in the books of Joshua and Judges in the Hebrew Bible. Neighboring southern Jordan, the geographic area known as "Edom," witnessed the emergence of the first historically-recorded state or kingdom level of social organization.[1] Thus, when considering the dynamics of social change in Israel/Palestine, scholars must consider developments and historical trajectories in the entire region (including Transjordan). The settlement of the tribes in Canaan has been a contentious issue, stimulating a number of distinctive models that attempt to meld the differing biblical accounts portrayed in these two books, the extrabiblical "historical" data, and archaeology to weave together the most likely model to describe what happened during the Late Bronze–Early Iron Age in the southern Levant. These "settlement" models have been described at length as the "Conquest Model,"[2] the "Peaceful Infiltration Model,"[3] the

---

1. Ø. S. LaBianca and R. W. Younker, "The Kingdoms of Ammon, Moab and Edom: The Archaeology of Society in Late Bronze/Iron Age Transjordan (ca. 1400–500 BCE)," *The Archaeology of Society in the Holy Land* (ed. T. E. Levy; London: Leicester University Press, 1998) 399–415.

2. W. F. Albright, "The Israelite Conquest of Canaan in the Light of Archaeology," *BASOR* 74 (1932) 11–23.

3. Y. Aharoni, "New Aspects of the Israelite Occupation in the North," *Near Eastern Archaeology in the Twentieth Century* (ed. J. A. Sanders; Garden City, N.Y.: Doubleday, 1970) 254–67; A. Alt, "Die Landnahme der Israeliten in Palästina," *Kleine Schriften* (Leipzig, 1925) 1.89–125.

"Peasant Revolt Model,"[4] the "Symbiosis Model,"[5] and most recently, the "Ethnogenesis Model."[6] This is not the place to review each of these models in detail, since the scholarly literature is replete with detailed discussions in support and refutation of each position. This essay is an attempt to explore the historical and archaeological data related to the Shasu pastoral nomads— one of the ethnic groups who were contemporaries of early Israel. This discussion has been prompted by the recent excavations of an Iron Age cemetery (Wadi Fidan 40; fig. 1) carried out by the authors, Levy and Adams, in 1997.[7] This paper is dedicated to David Noel Freedman, friend, colleague, and mentor, who has done so much to promote the interplay between archaeology, history, and the Hebrew Bible.

Ethnicity as it relates to the archaeological record is a contentious issue, not only in regard to the Late Bronze Age–Early Iron Age archaeological record of the Levant,[8] but in regard to the world archaeology scene in general.[9] In terms of the southern Levant, the Late Bronze–Early Iron Age interface represents an important period in which Egyptian epigraphic data, biblical narratives, and archaeological data can be used to explore the ethnic tapestry that existed in the region when early Israelite settlement took place. While the Hebrew Bible has been carefully curated and burnished into its present form since the late Iron Age,[10] it is the unchanging literary source that sets the stage for understanding the emergence of Israel in Canaan. While future discoveries of new epigraphic data relating directly to Israel during the Late Bronze–Early Iron Age may provide further details, at present the archaeological record provides the only source of new information that can help scholars understand the background against which early Israel developed. In this paper, we present new information concerning what we believe are the remains of an extensive cemetery in southern Jordan that

4. N. K. Gottwald, *The Tribes of Yahweh: A Sociology of the Religion of Liberated Israel, 1250–1050 B.C.E.* (New York: Orbis, 1979); G. E. Mendenhall, "The Hebrew Conquest of Palestine," *BA* 25 (1962) 66–87.

5. V. Fritz, "Conquest or Settlement? The Early Iron Age in Palestine," *BA* 50 (1987) 84–100.

6. T. E. Levy and A. F. C. Holl, "Migrations, Ethnogenesis, and Settlement Dynamics: Israelites in Iron Age Canaan and Shuwa-Arabs in the Chad Basin," *Journal of Anthropological Archaeology* 21 (2002) 83–118.

7. T. E. Levy, R. B. Adams, and R. Shafiq, "The Jabal Hamrat Fidan Project: Excavations at the Wadi Fidan 40 Cemetery, Jordan (1997)," *Levant* 31 (1999) 293–308.

8. W. G. Dever, "Ceramics, Ethnicity, and the Question of Israel's Origins," *BA* 58 (1995) 200–213.

9. S. Jones, *The Archaeology of Ethnicity: Constructing Identities in the Past and Present* (London: Routledge, 1997).

10. R. E. Friedman, *Who Wrote the Bible?* (New York: Summit, 1987).

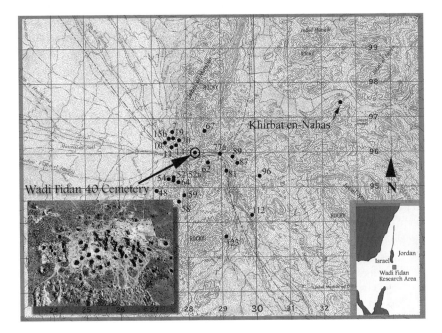

Fig. 1. Map of Research area.

belonged to the Shasu nomads and can be dated to the Early Iron Age II. While the suggestion that this cemetery belonged to the Shasu was made in an earlier paper,[11] here we explore some of the social dimensions reflected in the cemetery excavations. This is particularly germane to the discussion of earliest Israel, for some scholars, such as Anson Rainey, have gone so far as to suggest that "Israel was evidently one group among many Shasu who were moving out of the steppe lands to find their livelihood in areas that would permit them to obtain their own food."[12] While we do not necessarily sub-scribe to that view here, it highlights just how important the issue of the Shasu and the mosaic of contemporary south Levantine cultures is for tack-ling the problem of Israelite settlement in Canaan.

Who Were the Shasu?

The Shasu were a social group of nomads who are known from Egyptian texts, wall reliefs, and monuments dating from the 18th Dynasty (ca. 1550–

11. Levy, Adams, and Shafiq, "The Jabal Hamrat Fidan Project."
12. A. F. Rainey, "Israel in Merneptah's Inscription and Reliefs," *IEJ* 51 (2001) 57–75.

1295 B.C.E.) through the Third Intermediate Period (ca. 1069–747 B.C.E.). To date, the term Shasu is known only from Egyptian sources. Scholars differ in identifying the origin and identity of the Shasu. Even the derivation of the word *Shasu* is uncertain: it is related either to the Egyptian verb 'to wander' or to Semitic 'to plunder'.[13] According to Ward,[14] an Egyptian origin for the word seems more likely. Because the Egyptian sources report the Shasu from vast tracts of the southern Levant, it can be assumed that they were not an ethnic group tied to only one specific region. Rather, the Shasu seem to represent a social class of nomads who reflect an ancient equivalent of the term *Bedouin,* which crosscuts different ethnic groups and relates more to a generic socioeconomic subsistence organization devoted to pastoral nomadism than to ethnicity. Ward presents a detailed summary of all the sources that make reference to the Shasu. With regard to the region of Edom, he states:

> Another group of texts places the Shasu in S Transjordan. Short lists of place-names in Nubian temples of Amenhotep III and Ramesses II record six toponyms located in "the land of Shasu."[15] Those that can be identified are in the Negeb or Edom.[16] One of the six, Seir in Edom, is found elsewhere in connection with the Shasu. A monument of Ramesses II claims that he "has plundered the Shasu-land, captured the mountain of Seir"; a 19th Dynasty model letter mentions "the Shasu-tribes of Edom"; Ramesses III declares that he has "destroyed the Seirites among the tribes of the Shasu."[17] From the Egyptian viewpoint, then, the Shasu were a prominent part of the Edomite population.[18]

As we get closer to the Late Bronze–Early Iron Age interface and the period of direct concern to our research in the Jabal Hamrat Fidan region in Edom, the links between the Shasu nomads and Edom become clearer. For example, approximately 60 years after Ramesses II, during the 8th year of Merenptah, about 1206 B.C.E., the term "Edom" appears for the first time in *Papyrus Anastasi* VI (lines 51–61):

---

13. R. Giveon, *Les Bédouins Shosou des documents égyptiens* (Documenta et Monumenta Orientis Antiqui 22; Leiden: Brill, 1971); W. A. Ward, "The Shasu 'Bedouin': Notes on a Recent Publication," *Journal of the Economic and Social History of the Orient* 15 (1972) 35–60; M. Weippert, "Semitische Nomaden des zweiten Jahrtausends: Über die *Šꜣśw* der ägyptischen Quellen," *Bib* 55 (1974) 265–80, 427–33.

14. W. A. Ward, "Shasu," *ABD* 5.1165–67.

15. Giveon, *Les Bédouins Shosou,* docs. 6a, 16a.

16. K. A. Kitchen, "Some New Light on the Asiatic Wars of Ramesses II," *JEA* 50 (1964) 66–67; Weippert, "Semitische Nomaden," 270–71.

17. Giveon, *Les Bédouins Shosou,* docs. 25, 37, 38.

18. Ward, "Shasu."

We have finished with allowing the Shasu clansfolk of Edom to pass the fort of Merenptah that is in Succoth ["Tjeku"], to the pools (brkt) of Pi-Atum of Merenptah (that is/are) in Succoth, to keep them alive and to keep alive their livestock, by the will of Pharaoh, LPH, the good Sun of Egypt, along with names from the other days on which the fort of Merenptah that is in Succoth was passed [by such people . . .].[19]

K. A. Kitchen,[20] in his highly useful summary of Egyptian texts related to Transjordan and Edom in particular, garners useful evidence that links extrabiblical data with biblical texts related to developments around the tenth century B.C.E., the time when the WFD (Wadi Fidan District) 40 Cemetery described below was occupied. Accordingly, *Papyrus Moscow* 127[21] states, "Oh that I could send him [his local oppressor] off to Nahar(in), to fetch the hidden *tmrgn* with whom he had (previously) gone to those of Seir!" Kitchen[22] suggests that the term *tmrgn* is a Semitic loanword for 'guide, interpreter' and proposes that *Papyrus Moscow* 127 is close in date to the alleged flight of Hadad, the baby prince of Edom, into 21st-Dynasty Egypt after David's forces conquered Edom.[23]

The Range of Sources for Identifying Ancient Pastoralists in the Levant

For the southern Levant, perhaps the most important evidence for the existence of pastoral social groups during the Bronze and Iron Ages is found in textual records such as (a) the Hebrew Bible,[24] (b) the Egyptian documents,[25] and (c) Egyptian monuments.[26] Texts provide the historical data for giving the emic evidence of names and places linked to the ancient pastoralists of the Levant. Another source for identifying pastoralism and pastoral nomadism in the archaeological record is archaeozoological remains. There is

19. Text: A. H. Gardiner, *Late-Egyptian Miscellanies, Vol. 7* (Bibliotheca Aegyptiaca; Brussels: Édition de la Fondation égyptologique Reine Élisabeth, 1937). Translations: e.g., *ANET,* 259 with notes; R. A. Caminos, *Late-Egyptian Miscellanies* (London: Oxford University Press, 1954).

20. K. A. Kitchen, "The Egyptian Evidence on Ancient Jordan," *Early Edom and Moab: The Beginning of the Iron Age in Southern Jordan* (ed. P. Bienkowski; Sheffield: Collis, 1992) 27.

21. R. A. Caminos, *A Tale of Woe: From a Hieratic Papyrus in the A. S. Pushkin Museum of Fine Arts in Moscow* (Oxford: Griffith Institute, Ashmolean Museum, 1977) 66–69.

22. Kitchen, "Egyptian Evidence on Ancient Jordan," 27.

23. 1 Kgs 11:14–22.

24. E.g., Amalekites, Kenites, and Midianites.

25. Giveon, *Les Bédouins Shosou.*

26. Cf. R. Giveon, "The Shosu of the Late XXth Dynasty," *JARCE* 8 (1969–70) 51–53.

a wide range of issues and techniques that archaeozoologists use to recon-
struct pastoral-oriented economies.[27] Some of these include the identification of the types of animals exploited, the structure of livestock herds based
on the minimum number of individuals (MNI) represented in faunal collections, and the age of animals at death to determine the hunting capabilities
of groups, the origins of domestication, and the specific type of livestock
exploitation. All of these aspects of archaeozoology play a central part in determining the socioeconomic structure of pastoral and pastoral nomadic
communities.

Finally, the material "fingerprint" of pastoral groups—the material residue of these people—provides important and perhaps the most ubiquitous
information for identifying these groups in the past. Ethnoarchaeology offers
an important source for establishing models for identifying the archaeological variables that can be used to study pastoral-based societies in all their
dimensions, such as continuous versus ephemeral occupation, abandonment
processes, nomadic grazing routes, and mortuary behavior, among others.
Some of the material features include campsites, hearths, and stone arcs representative of tent locations.

The Difficulty in Tracing Nomads in the Archaeological Record

In tackling the problem of identifying and studying pastoralism and pastoral nomadism in the archaeological record, it is essential to conceptualize
them in socioeconomic terms. Most anthropologists perceive pastoralism, in
all its forms, as rooted in economic activities.[28] For our purposes, we follow
Khazanov's[29] and Bar-Yosef and Khazanov's[30] definition that states:

> pastoralism may be conceived of as a mobile and extensive animal husbandry
> not necessarily divergent from agriculture. However, from the economic
> point of view, pure pastoral nomads should be defined as a distinctive type of

27. S. J. M. Davis, *The Archaeology of Animals* (New Haven: Yale University Press,
1987); C. Grigson, "Plough and Pasture in the Early Economy of the Southern Levant,"
The Archaeology of Society in the Holy Land (ed. T. E. Levy; London: Leicester University
Press, 1998) 245–68; B. Hesse and P. Wapnish, *Animal Bone Archeology: From Objectives to
Analysis* (Washington, D.C.: Taraxacum, 1985).

28. T. J. Barfield, *The Nomadic Alternative* (Englewood Cliffs, N.J.: Prentice Hall,
1993); O. Bar-Yosef and A. Khazanov (eds.), *Pastoralism in the Levant: Archaeological Materials in Anthropological Perspectives* (Madison, Wisc.: Prehistory Press, 1992); W. Lancaster,
The Rwala Bedouin Today (2nd ed.; Prospect Heights, Ill.: Waveland, 1997); E. Marx, "Are
There Pastoral Nomads in the Middle East?" *Pastoralism in the Levant*, 255–60.

29. A. M. Khazanov, *Nomads and the Outside World* (2nd ed.; Madison, Wisc.: University of Wisconsin Press, 1994).

30. Bar-Yosef and Khazanov, *Pastoralism in the Levant*, 2.

food-producing economy. By this definition, extensive mobile pastoralism is the predominant activity through which the majority of the population is drawn into periodic migrations in order to maintain herds all year round within a system of free-range pastures. Contrary to all other forms of pastoralism, pure pastoral nomadism is characterized by the absence of agriculture even in a supplementary capacity.

This broad economic definition of pastoralism and pastoral nomadism is useful for framing the nature of pastoral-based communities encountered in the archaeological record.

Numerous scholars have grappled with the problem of the visibility of nomadic communities in the archaeological record.[31] Perhaps V. Gordon Childe[32] said it best: "The failure to recognize prehistoric settlement sites as belonging to pure pastoralists is not any proof that such did not exist." In the deserts of the southern Levant, the visibility of pastoral nomads in the archaeological record has been a point of debate out of which two schools of thought have emerged. On the one hand there are the scholars represented primarily by S. Rosen[33] who believe that the absence of material remains is indicative of no occupation by pastoral-based peoples. An alternative perspective is represented by Finkelstein,[34] who suggests that there "is no possibility of periods of human 'void' . . ." in these desert areas. As Finkelstein and Perevolotsky[35] point out, during the nineteenth century there were thousands of Bedouin pastoralists living in the Negev and Sinai, and yet, at the end of the twentieth century, it is difficult to recognize their remains. This problem is highlighted even more by the long history of Bedouin occupation in the Negev, where oral histories document over twelve major tribal wars in the region from the seventeenth through nineteenth centuries.[36] Virtually none of the rich history of these pastoral nomads is preserved in the material record of the Negev today. While there is logic in Rosen's position, that without hard archaeological facts it must be assumed there was an absence of nomadic occupation in a region, here we are inclined to take a more measured position between Rosen and Finkelstein. Why could not there be a period

---

31. H. Crawford, "The Mechanics of the Obsidian Trade," *Antiquity* 52 (1978) 129–32; E. E. Herzfeld, *Archaeological History of Iran* (London: British Academy, 1935).

32. V. G. Childe, *Man Makes Himself* (London: Watts, 1936) 81.

33. S. A. Rosen, "Nomads in Archaeology: A Response to Finkelstein and Perevolotsky," *BASOR* 287 (1992) 75–85.

34. I. Finkelstein, "Invisible Nomads: A Rejoinder," *BASOR* 287 (1992) 87–88; I. Finkelstein and A. Perevolotsky, "Processes of Sedentarization and Nomadization in the History of Sinai and the Negev," *BASOR* 278 (1990) 67.

35. Ibid.

36. C. Bailey, "The Negev in the Nineteenth Century: Reconstructing History from Bedouin Oral Traditions," *Asian and African Studies* 14 (1980) 35–80.

when nomadic communities ceased to exist in a region? It is always danger-
ous to state emphatically that "there is no possibility" for something to have
occurred in the past. Migration, genocide, plagues, and other catastrophes
can always decimate a human population. With new research designs and
new exploratory methods, new discoveries can always be made that shed light
on archaeological problems such as ancient pastoral nomadic communities.

Identifying nomadic communities is notoriously difficult, as highlighted
by the debate between I. Finkelstein and S. Rosen, which focuses on the
archaeology of western Palestine. A. J. Frendo[37] has provided a very useful
summary of some of the reasons it is so difficult to identify nomads in the
Near Eastern archaeological record. These include: (1) nomadic remains may
be covered by sediment deposition; (2) fences used to construct corrals may
have been made of shrubs and other forms of vegetation (rather than stones)
that do not survive the ravages of time; (3) natural erosion processes may remove evidence of ephemeral tent camps; (4) cultural formation processes by
human activities may remove evidence of nomadic sites; and (5) some archaeologists may not be familiar with the material correlates of nomadic societies and may fail to identify them in the field.

As will be shown here, until recently,[38] no scholar had suggested that
there was archaeological evidence for the existence of the Shasu nomads
known from historical sources to have occupied ancient Edom. Now, after
careful field surveys and systematic excavations in one part of Edom—the
Jabal Hamrat Fidan—it is possible to begin an "archaeology of nomads"
and build a case for identifying the Shasu in Edom. This identification is
rapidly gaining acceptance by researchers studying the Iron Age in southern
Jordan.[39]

Some of the archaeological correlates of pastoral nomadic community activities in the desert regions of the Levant include campsites, cemeteries,
open-air cult places, rock inscriptions and drawings, corral walls, stone enclo-
sures, hearths, stone arcs, and other features. For the purposes of the Jabal
Hamrat Fidan research area, the categories of cemeteries, tent remains, and
open-air cultic installations provide some of the most important parallels for
isolating material remains belonging to pastoral nomads in the archaeological
record of the southern Levant.

Perhaps the earliest Levantine cemeteries that can be linked to nomadic
populations are the approximately 21 fields of *Nawamis,* stone-built burial

37. A. J. Frendo, "The Capabilities and Limitations of Ancient Near Eastern Nomadic
Archaeology," *Or* 65 (1996) 1–23.
38. Levy, Adams, and Shafiq, "The Jabal Hamrat Fidan Project."
39. Cf. P. Bienkowski and E. van der Steen, "Tribes, Trade, and Towns: A New Frame-
work for the Late Iron Age in Southern Jordan and the Negev," *BASOR* 323 (2001) 21–47.

structures found in the Sinai Desert[40] dating to the end of the Chalcolithic and Early Bronze IA. Conceivably, the most significant indicator that these mortuary sites belonged to a nomadic community is their remote location and isolation from settlement sites. Since the camel was probably not domesticated until sometime during the end of the Late Bronze Age,[41] it is assumed that the nomadic communities that used these mortuary sites were sheep/goat pastoralists. Unlike the vast sand deserts of the Sahara or the Arabian Peninsula, which could be penetrated only with the camel, the deserts of the Levant (Sinai, Negev, southern Jordan) are relatively small geographical areas, not far from the Mediterranean environmental zones, and contain numerous fresh water springs that are readily available for herd animals such as sheep and goats. Thus, the presence of the Early Bronze IA *Nawamis* in the Sinai and earlier Chalcolithic settlements in the northern Negev point to a long history of pastoralism in the deserts of the Levant.[42]

An additional source of nomad mortuary evidence comes from the hundreds of Bedouin Arab cemeteries found throughout the deserts of the southern Levant.[43] These cemeteries provide an important index of the way that cemeteries of nomadic populations change with the degree of sedentarization of the community that uses them. Consider, for example, the northern Negev desert, where thousands of Bedouin were encouraged to settle in permanent villages and towns established in the wake of the Israeli army's withdrawal from the Sinai in 1979, when a number of air bases were constructed in the Negev. Each year following the resettlement of the Bedouin, mortuary monuments changed radically, from the simple, traditional placement of two natural rocks at the head and foot of the interred to well-built brick structures covered with plaster and marble and decorated with finely carved inscriptions with Arabic calligraphy. Thus, cemeteries belonging to nomadic communities may provide a particularly clear index to the degree of sedentarization among those social groups.

The Iron Age in Southern Jordan

The archaeological evidence for occupation in southern Jordan, south of the Wadi Hasa, in the area commonly referred to as Edom, is both sparse and difficult to date. Outside of the few well-known sites (most of which were

---

40. O. Bar-Yosef et al., "The Orientation of Nawamis Entrances in Southern Sinai: Expressions of Religious Belief and Seasonality?" *TA* 10 (1983) 52–60.

41. Grigson, "Plough and Pasture."

42. T. E. Levy, "The Emergence of Specialized Pastoralism in the Southern Levant," *World Archaeology* 15 (1983) 15–36.

43. E. Marx, "The Tribe as a Unit of Subsistence: Nomadic Pastoralism in the Middle East," *American Anthropologist* 79 (1977) 343–63.

excavated decades ago, such as Busayrah, Tawilan, and Umm el-Biyara), few others of any significance have been excavated in recent years. Over the last few decades, new information about the Iron Age occupation of southern Jordan has come largely from a number of survey projects both on the Edomite and Kerak Plateaus and in the Wadi Arabah: the Wadi al-Hasa Survey,[44] the Kerak Plateau Survey,[45] and the Southern Ghors and Northeast Arabah Survey Project.[46] The results of these surveys have suggested that the region of southern Jordan, far from being devoid of sites, was in fact quite densely settled at various times throughout the Iron Age. Largely as a result of these surveys, there has been considerable debate about the nature of this occupation, its relationship to the preceding Late Bronze Age, and the overall picture of southern Jordan in relationship to other parts of the southern Levant during this formative period. The assertions made by the various surveyors was that the quality of the data from these new sites supported the view that many of them were occupied during both the Late Bronze Age and the Iron Age and that some spanned both periods. The primary basis for almost all of the site dating came from the survey pottery, which has been controversial because there has been concern about whether the data were correctly interpreted.

A limited reconnaissance of several key sites from two of these surveys in 1994 led to trial excavations of the best-preserved sites, Khirbat Dubab and Ash-Shorabat,[47] the results of which cast serious doubt on the overall results of the surveys in correctly identifying the Late Bronze Age–Iron Age transition and the earliest Iron Age of southern Jordan. The findings from the soundings of these two sites suggested limited Iron Age II occupation at Ash-Shorabat, and at Khirbat Dubab no in situ Iron Age remains were found in the trial trenches, but there was evidence of residual Iron Age II sherds from surface contexts in the slope wash from the Khirbet. As a result of the findings of these excavations, Bienkowski has restudied the survey pottery from Khirbet Dubab collected by the Kerak Plateau Survey Project and concluded that in most cases the ceramics from the survey were simply "misidentified and misdated."[48] In the case of Ash-Shorabat, there seems to have been a

44. B. MacDonald, *The Wadi al-Hasa Archaeological Survey 1979–83: West-Central Jordan* (Waterloo, Ont.: Wilfrid Laurier University Press, 1988).

45. J. M. Miller (ed.), *Archaeological Survey of the Kerak Plateau* (ASOR Archaeological Reports 1; Atlanta: Scholars Press, 1991).

46. B. MacDonald, *The Southern Ghors and Northeast ʿArabah Archaeological Survey, Vol. 5* (Sheffield Archaeological Monographs 5; Sheffield: Collis, 1992).

47. P. Bienkowski and R. B. Adams, "Soundings at Ash-Shorabat and Khirbat Dubab in the Wadi Hasa, Jordan: The Pottery," *Levant* 31 (1999) 149–72; P. Bienkowski et al., "Soundings at Ash-Shorabat and Khirbat Dubab in the Wadi Hasa, Jordan: The Stratigraphy," *Levant* 29 (1997) 41–70.

48. Bienkowski and van der Steen, "Tribes, Trade, and Towns," 259.

clear misdating of later Iron Age II pottery to Iron I, based largely on the coarse fabrics.

As a result of the recent reexaminations of the data from these surveys, our understanding of the earliest phase of the Iron Age in southern Jordan is scarcely better off than it was previously. Given the unreliable results from more than a decade of survey in the region, it is not yet possible to make a claim for Early Iron Age occupation in most of southern Jordan or to understand the relationship between the emerging Iron Age states of the region in terms of the Late Bronze Age of the southern Levant. As yet no clear continuity between these periods has been adequately documented.

Iron Age Occupation in the Faynan Region, Southern Jordan

The one exception to the above is the evidence now beginning to appear from the Faynan region, the results of which are the best argument yet for the reoccupation of southern Jordan in the Iron Age, following the scant evidence for occupations during the Middle and Late Bronze Ages. As early as 1986, a study of the Iron Age pottery of the Faynan region by Hart and Knauf revised Knauf's earlier dating of the pottery to the "Early Iron Age"[49] and instead suggested three groupings in the Iron Age pottery from this region. The first group was proposed to belong to the seventh-century Edomite phases and included similar types to those already known from the Edomite sites on the plateau. The second group was "Jordanian Negebite" pottery, which was a coarse, handmade pottery with similarities to wares found in the Negev and on the plateau. The third was tentatively called "non-Edomite Iron Age" and included forms and fabrics that were distinctly different from the standard Edomite assemblages known at that time.[50] Hart suggested that the pottery was likely earlier, but later he preferred the term "Early Edomite," since in his view "the shapes are not completely unrelated to Edomite forms, are less precise and difficult to classify."[51]

Since 1998, further details of the Iron Age occupation of the Faynan basin have been revealed by the Wadi Faynan Landscape Survey. In particular, the survey results indicate that the two groups of Iron Age pottery first identified by Hart and Knauf are represented throughout the survey area and that

---

49. A. Hauptmann, G. Weisberger, and E. A. Knauf, "Archäometallurgische und bergbauarchäologische Untersuchungen im Gebiet von Fenan, Wadi Arabah (Jordanien)," *Der Anschnitt* 37 (1985) 163–95.

50. S. Hart, *The Archaeology of the Land of Edom* (Sydney: Macquarie University Press, 1989) 124–25; S. Hart and E. A. Knauf, "Wadi Feinan Iron Age Pottery," *Newsletter of the Institute of Archaeology and Anthropology, Yarmouk University* 1 (1986) 9–10.

51. Hart, *Archaeology of the Land of Edom*, 125.

in some cases they appear in isolation from each other, suggesting a chronological distinction. This is particularly clear in Wadi Faynan Area 424 and in
cuttings made in erosion sections where "non-Edomite Iron Age" pottery is
found in conjunction with copper-smelting installations.[52] A detailed analysis of this material is now underway in preparation for the final report, but
preliminary work on both the typology and the fabric analysis suggests a clear
distinction between these two groups of Iron Age pottery, with the "non-
Edomite Iron Age" pottery probably relating to the earliest phases of Iron
Age II (that is, the tenth through eighth centuries).

This early phase of Iron Age pottery is supported by finds of similar
pottery from other sites in the region, including the excavations at Barqa
el-Hetiye[53] and at Khirbet en-Nahas.[54] At Barqa el-Hetiye, excavation of a
multiroomed mudbrick/stone building revealed an extensive collection of ceramics very similar to the "non-Edomite Iron Age pottery" from the region
of Khirbet Faynan, as well as good examples of painted Midianite wares. Fritz
suggested an Iron Age I date for this structure based on similarities of the
collared-rim jars (CRJs) to Palestinian pottery repertoires and also on the
basis of the presence of the Midianite wares in the assemblage. However, as
Bienkowski rightly notes, the CRJs, as shown by Herr,[55] are also at home in
Iron Age II, and the evidence for clear chronological dating of Midianite
wares has not yet been established.[56] Herr's well-stratified evidence from Tall
al-Umayri supports the continued use of CRJs down to the end of the Iron
Age II, and definitive analysis of stratified CRJs from other sites may eventually support his preliminary findings. Indeed, CRJs as well as Midianite wares
appear in the Faynan Landscape Survey pottery but have not been interpreted as evidence of Iron Age I occupation. Clearly the most important factor in the Barqa site is the radiocarbon date, which points to a ninth-century
B.C.E. date (see table 1).

At Khirbet en-Nahas a small stone and slag-built building produced a
smaller sample of ceramics, from excavations within and outside the structure, which Fritz dated to Iron Age II.[57] The radiocarbon evidence from this

52. G. W. Barker et al., "Environment and Land Use in the Wadi Faynan, Southern
Jordan: The Third Season of Geoarchaeology and Landscape Archaeology (1998)," *Levant*
31 (1999) 255–92.

53. V. Fritz, "Vorbericht über die Grabungen in Barqa el-Hetiye im Gebiet von Fenan,
Wadi el-Araba (Jordanien) 1990," *ZDPV* 110 (1994) 125–50.

54. V. Fritz, "Ergebnisse einer Sondage in Hirbet en-Nahas, Wadi el-ʿAraba (Jordanien)," *ZDPV* 112 (1996) 1–9.

55. L. G. Herr, D. R. Clark, and W. C. Trenchard, "Madaba Plains Project: Excavations at Tall Al-ʿUmayri, 2000," *Annual of the Department of Antiquities of Jordan* 45 (2001)
237–52.

56. Bienkowski and van der Steen, "Tribes, Trade, and Towns," 261.

57. Fritz, "Ergebnisse einer Sondage."

**Table 1. Radiocarbon Dates from Two Iron Age Sites
in the Faynan Basin**

Site	Source	Sample Ref.	Radiocarbon Date Age BP	Radiocarbon Date Calibrated BC (1σ)
Barqa el-Hetiye	House 2	HD 13977	2743 ± 23	905–835
Khirbet en-Nahas	House 1	HD 13978	2704 ± 52	900–805

building points to a similar date, although the ceramic evidence is less clear, since both "Edomite painted wares" and "non-Edomite Iron Age pottery" occur in this excavation sample (table 1). (This may be a result of problems in the excavation and mixing of phases at this site.)

All of these data were also reinforced by the evidence from the Jabal Hamrat Fidan Archaeological Survey in 1998,[58] where evidence of numerous Iron Age sites throughout the wadi yielded both the later "Edomite Iron Age" and the "non-Edomite Iron Age" pottery, which matched the results from the wider Faynan basin. Many of the Iron Age sites found in the survey also contained evidence nearby for small-scale copper smelting installations, although one site known as Nelson Glueck's "Khirbat Hamra Ifdan"[59] may well have been a strategic post guarding the southern approach to Khirbat en-Nahas.

The results of the 1998 intensive, systematic, pedestrian archaeological survey carried out along the Wadi Fidan were instrumental in demonstrating the nomadic nature of the local settlement pattern along this important drainage.[60] A total of 24 Iron Age sites were found along the 4.5 km long (× 1 km wide) survey area. There is a lack of developed settlement sites in this region, which represents the "gateway" to the copper-ore-rich Faynan district. Instead, the sites are dominated by cemeteries (N = 7, including WFD 40), small-scale metal processing sites without building structures (N = 4), a large campsite, and other smaller sites. This is not to say that Iron Age settlement sites do not exist in the Faynan district. Two of the most famous Iron

58. T. E. Levy et al., "Early Metallurgy, Interaction, and Social Change: The Jabal Hamrat Fidan (Jordan) Research Design and 1998 Archaeological Survey: Preliminary Report," *Annual of the Department of Antiquities of Jordan* 45 (2001) 1–31.

59. R. B. Adams, "Romancing the Stones: New Light on Glueck's Survey of Eastern Palestine as a Result of Recent Work by the Wadi Fidan Project," in *Early Edom and Moab: The Beginning of the Iron Age in Southern Jordan* (ed. P. Bienkowski; Sheffield Archaeological Monographs 7; Sheffield: Collis, 1992) 177–86.

60. Levy et al., "Early Metallurgy."

Age sites in the region, Khirbat en-Nahas[61] and Khirbat Faynan (biblical Punon),[62] provide evidence of extensive building complexes that no doubt indicate permanent settlement. However, WFD 40, with over 3,500 well-built mortuary monuments, is isolated and relatively far from these large Iron Age settlement and industrial sites. The dichotomy between the Wadi Fidan "nomadic" Iron Age settlement pattern and the patterns that characterize the main Faynan Valley and the Wadi Ghuwayb where Khirbat en-Nahas is situated are characteristic of the relationship between settled communities and nomads known from the Near Eastern ethnographic record.[63]

By far the largest Iron Age site in the survey area of the Wadi Fidan was the Wadi Fidan 40 Cemetery. This site has been known for many years, but the dating had been in question until the 1997 excavations of the Jabal Hamrat Fidan Project, which successfully dated the site to the early phases of Iron Age II. The results of the excavation provide the first tentative archaeological evidence for the Shasu nomads, known from the textual records.

The Wadi Fidan 40 Cemetery: Preliminary Spatial Analysis of an Iron Age Nomad Cemetery

The Wadi Fidan 40 Cemetery is located on a Pleistocene terrace along the north bank of the Wadi Fidan some 20 m above the present drainage channel. Based on the on-site survey of the grave structures visible on the site surface, the cemetery is estimated to extend over an area of ca. 17,600 m². The surface is densely packed with the remains of circular grave structures (ca. 5 structures : 25 m²), making it possible to estimate the total number of graves represented in the cemetery at about 3,500 mortuary structures. The cemetery was first identified and sampled by R. B. Adams in 1989[64] and was initially thought to be linked to the Wadi Fidan 4 Early Bronze Age I village. However, the first systematic excavations at the site conducted by T. E. Levy and Adams in 1997 exposed an area of approximately 1,505.65 m², gained a representative sample of the cemetery site, and showed conclusively that the cemetery dates to the Iron Age, rather than the Early Bronze Age.

The discovery of iron ornaments and a radiocarbon determination from one of the best-preserved tombs date the cemetery to the Iron Age. The results of this analysis undertaken by Beta Analytic, Inc., come from Wadi

61. T. E. Levy et al., "Nahas (Khirbet en-)," *Archaeological Encyclopedia of the Holy Land* (ed. A. Negev and S. Gibson; New York: Continuum, 2001) 361; Fritz, "Ergebnisse einer Sondage."

62. Barker et al., "Environment and Land Use."

63. Khazanov, *Nomads and the Outside World*; Levy and Holl, "Migrations, Ethnogenesis."

64. Adams, "Romancing the Stones."

Table 2. Results of Radiometric Dating of a
Fruit Sample from Grave 92

Sample Number	Measured C14 Age	C13/C12 Ratio	Conventional C14	Calibrated results intercept of 2 sigma 95% probability	Calibrated radio-carbon age with calibration curve	1 sigma 68% probability
Beta-111366	2800 ± 70 BP	–25.0 0/00	2800 ± 70 BP	cal BC 1130–815	Cal BC 925	cal BC 1015–845

Fidan 40 Cemetery, Area A, Grave 92, Locus 531, Basket: 2133 + 2157 (table 2). The material consisted of pomegranate seeds that were pretreated using acid/alkali/acid.

More detailed descriptions of the grave structures, mortuary practices, burial position, grave goods, preservation, and skeletal remains can be found in our preliminary report.[65] For our purposes here, we wish to present a short overview of the character of the cemetery and preliminary implications for understanding the social organization reflected in the mortuary remains. Very briefly, each burial monument was constructed for one individual and consists of a circular pit that was dug approximately 1 m below the surface. At the bottom of the pit, a stone-lined cist grave was prepared for the deceased, the dimensions of which were made according to the size of the deceased. The cist walls and capstones were all made of hewn stones. Once the capstones were placed over the deceased (who, depending on gender, was usually buried with wooden bowls, beads, iron and copper jewelry, pendants, etc.), a thin layer of pise was smeared over the capstones to seal the burial. The hole containing the cist was then filled with sediment, and a ring or circle of wadi cobbles (usually dolorite) was placed around the edge of the hole to mark the grave. Sometimes a series of flat wadi cobbles were used to make a paved surface inside this circular grave marker. The diameter of these grave circles varies from 80–99 cm to over 2.60 m. It is the preponderance of these grave circles on the site surface that allows us to make the remarkable estimates for the number of individuals possibly buried in the cemetery.

The broad excavation exposure revealed a total of 62 grave structures. As seen in the plan illustrating the layout of these graves (fig. 2), it is possible to detect four clusters of grave circles in the excavation area. Determining tight clusters of graves based on rigorous analytical methods is beyond the scope of this study. To determine the grave clusters accurately, a detailed GIS analysis of the cemetery is needed, using spatial analytical techniques based

65. Levy, Adams, and Shafiq, "The Jabal Hamrat Fidan Project."

on variations of Nearest Neighbor Analysis and other tools for mapping density.[66] For this preliminary study, we simply work with the visual impression made by the grave circles in association with preliminary plots of the grave goods found in the cemetery. To ensure that all small burial goods, human remains, animal bones, and other small objects were retrieved from the cemetery, all sediment from each grave was sieved through 3 and 5 mm mesh dry-sieves. If small beads were found, excavation strategies were changed and the smaller mesh was used. In what follows, a brief description of the spatial distribution of the grave goods found in the cemetery is given in an effort to determine grave clustering and the implications for understanding the social organization and nature of the society that used the cemetery.

The Wadi Fidan District 40 Bead Assemblage

The most ubiquitous grave offerings found in the WFD 40 Cemetery are beads. A large assemblage totaling about 2,004 beads that were strung in necklaces, bracelets, and anklets were found in the excavated graves.[67] The beads are made from a wide variety of minerals as well as bone, coral, shell, and, very occasionally, glass. The primary minerals used included (in order by number found) onyx, carnelian, limestone, Amazon stone, Egyptian alabaster (calcite), chalk, agate, apatite, amber, marble, quartz, jasper, sandstone, chrysoprase, feldspar, and haematite, all of which can be found locally in the Faynan region. However, it should be noted that the one peculiarity of the mineral assemblage used for the beads is the nearly complete lack of copper minerals, which are so readily available in the Faynan area. With the exception of two chrysoprase beads, no other copper minerals were found. This is in contrast to other periods of occupation in the region, when copper minerals were used extensively. During the Early Bronze Age, the village at Wadi Fidan 4 on the opposite bank of the Wadi Fidan saw the use of copper ore extensively for the production of copper beads, and during the Pre-Pottery Neolithic, copper minerals were used for beads as well as pigments at the nearby village at Wadi Fidan 1. Both of these examples indicate that settled peoples of the region made use of these copper minerals, in contrast to the Iron Age populations of the Wadi Fidan 40 Cemetery, raising the possibility that this population was not interested in the wealth of copper ores available nearby.

There is a wide variety of shapes and sizes of beads represented in the assemblage, attesting to a varied industry of production techniques used in

66. A. Mitchell, *The ESRI Guide to GIS Analysis—Volume 1: Geographic Patterns & Relationships* (Redlands: ESRI, 1999).

67. L. Harris, *The Social Archaeology of Beads: Evidence from the Wadi Fidan 40 Cemetery, Southern Jordan* (B.A. thesis, University of Bristol, 2000).

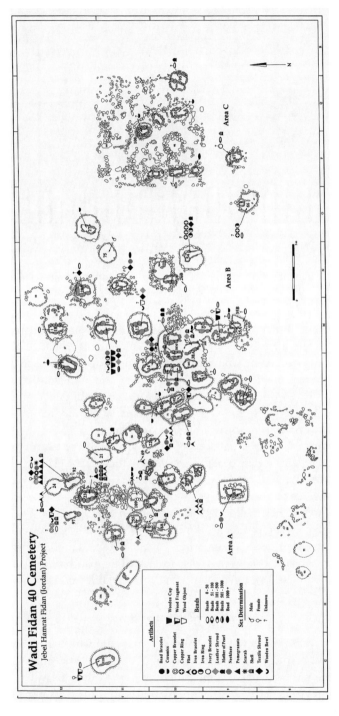

Fig. 2. Distribution map of graves and artifacts from Wadi Fidan District 40.

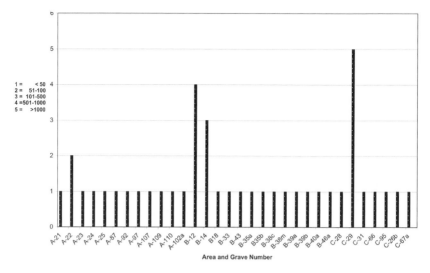

Fig. 3. Histogram showing number of beads by area and grave (in increments of < 50, 51–100, 101–500, 501–1000, and > 1000).

their shaping and manufacture. The technique of shaping no doubt varied according to the materials being used, because the bone, shell, coral, limestone, and Amazon stone would have been quite easily shaped due to their softness, whereas other minerals such as quartz and carnelian were likely more difficult to work due to their relative hardness. In general, different minerals and materials seem to have been formed in specific shapes, perhaps reflecting the ease (or not) of working the material.

By far the most interesting aspect of the bead assemblage was the presence of a small number of glass beads. Altogether there were 14 glass beads from graves 12, 14, 29, and 92. This small sample was composed of a variety of colors from green to green-blue, yellow, black, and white, and were primarily small, disk-shaped beads, although the largest two were spherical. The largest bead was actually composite, having inclusions of bone as raised relief. The origin of these glass beads among what is assumed to be a mobile population is uncertain, but the beads are similar to many Egyptian beads of the early first millennium, and an Egyptian origin cannot be ruled out.

The Distribution of Beads

There were 32 graves (or 51.6 %) that were found with beads (fig. 2). In this preliminary study, we are not presenting a detailed spatial analysis of the beads based on their material composition. At a later time, this will be an important source of data for identifying variation among the graves. In this very

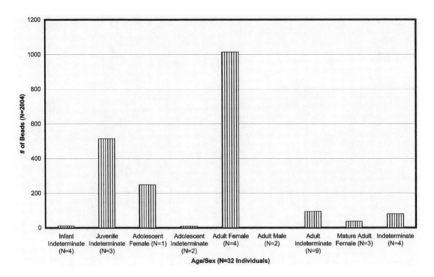

Fig. 4. Histogram: beads by age and sex (infant—indeterminate age, juvenile—indeterminate age, adolescent female, adolescent—indeterminate, adult female, adult male, adult indeterminate, adult—mature, adult—mature indeterminate).

preliminary study, we are focusing on the numerical distribution of beads in the cemetery. Figure 3 illustrates the distribution of beads by grave and excavation area. There seems little doubt that these beads were part of necklaces, most of which probably belonged to women, that were buried with the deceased. Figure 4 shows the distribution of beads by age and sex found in the WFD 40 Cemetery, the vast majority of which are associated with four adult females, three mature adult females, and one adolescent female. Unsexed juveniles (N = 3) and indeterminate adults (N = 9) make up the next categories with large numbers of beads. It is likely that, if DNA studies are carried out on the human remains associated with these graves, they also will turn out to be females. In fact, only two adult males were found with beads (N = 3 beads), making it highly probable that beads are a good marker for female gender in the WFD 40 archaeological record. Accordingly, the distribution of beads was divided into the following categories: < 50, 51–100, 101–500, 501–1000, and >1000. Only 4 graves included more than 50 beads [Graves 12 (N = 511), 14 (N = 249), 22 (N = 68), and 29 (N = 1,008)]. The remaining 28 graves had an average of 6 beads per grave with a range of between 1 and 45 beads. Of the 4 graves with more than 50 beads, 2 have been definitively identified as female. The remaining 2 graves contained skeletons whose sex cannot be identified but who were most likely female, based on evidence presented here. Of the 28 graves with less than 50

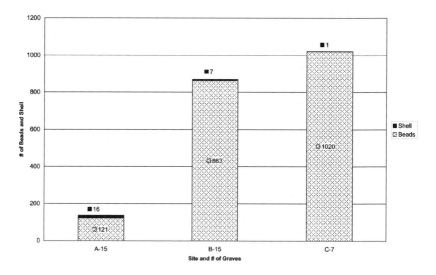

Fig. 5. Histogram of bead materials by frequency.

beads, 2 were identified as male and 6 as female, 16 were unidentified, and 4 were graves that did not contain human remains.

As grave goods, what do the beads represent? How many beads are necessary to assume that a necklace was included as a grave offering? While it is tempting to assume that each grave containing beads implies that the deceased was buried with a necklace, we can only be sure that 4 graves contain more than 50 beads. These may be the only graves that can be interpreted as containing necklaces. How should we define the remaining graves with less than 50 beads? The remaining graves can be divided into two meaningful categories: 25 graves include less than 10 beads, and 3 graves were found with 28 to 45 beads. We know that Bedouin (men, women, children) often wear several beads on a string around their necks or wrists as a kind of amulet.[68] One group of beads (N = 23) was found in Grave 14 on a string resting on one of the arms of the deceased, suggesting that it was a bracelet. Thus, here we assume that graves with >100 beads represent the presence of necklaces, and those with <100 beads indicate amulets that may have been worn as a necklace/amulet or bracelet. Can the beads be used to infer social prestige? Most of the raw materials used in the manufacture of the WFD 40

68. A. Musil, *Manners and Customs of the Rwala Bedouin* (New York: American Geographical Society, 1927); S. Weir, *The Bedouin: Aspects of the Material Culture of the Bedouin of Jordan* (London: World of Islam Festival, 1976).

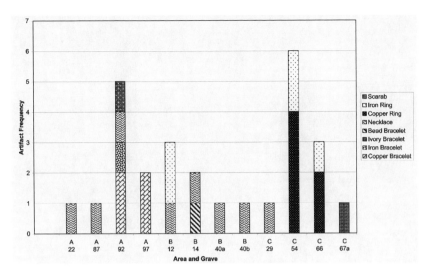

Fig. 6. Histogram: ornamentation (bracelets, necklaces, rings, scarabs) by excavation area and grave.

beads (quartz, carnelian, onyx and other agates, amazonite and other materials) are from rock sources that are locally available. The necklace buried with Grave 92 (fig. 8)[69] included a Middle Bronze IIB "Hyksos" scarab, which we interpret as an heirloom. However, the lack of beads made from precious metals or minerals argues against using beads to infer the kind of complex social organization associated with urban societies. Thus, the social interpretation of the beads cannot be separated from a multiview study of the entire material culture assemblage represented in the cemetery. Accordingly, there is little architectural variation within the cemetery (except on the basis of the age of the deceased), and at this time we have not found evidence of a rigid social hierarchy represented by the mortuary remains. However, as seen in fig. 5, the fact that the majority of the bead assemblage was found in graves from the Area A and B clusters of burials suggests that individuals from these clusters may be women with relatively more prestige than those found in Area C in the WFD 40 Cemetery. However, this assumed "ranking" in prestige is impressionistic and the differences between Areas A and B so minor that we assume some kind of "egalitarian" principle was at work in the burial tradition at WFD 40.

69. Levy, Adams, and Shafiq, "The Jabal Hamrat Fidan Project," 299; A. Rowe, *A Catalogue of Egyptian Scarabs, Scaraboids and Amulets in the Palestine Archaeology Museum* (Cairo: Imprimerie de Institut Francais, 1936) 331.

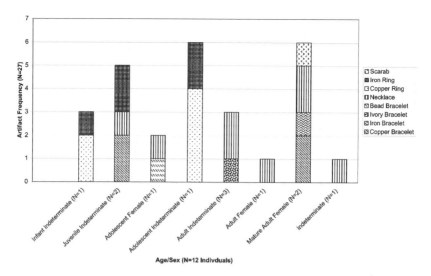

Fig. 7. Histogram: ornamentation (bracelets, necklaces, rings, scarabs) by age and sex.

The Distribution of Ornaments

For the purpose of this preliminary study, ornamentation refers to: metal rings and bracelets (made from both copper and iron) and necklaces or bracelets from beads already discussed above. Metal jewelry (bracelets and rings) may be the most unambiguous evidence of "wealth" in the WFD 40 Cemetery. Here we discuss the metal ornaments. Four graves were found with bracelets (for arms or legs) and 3 with metal finger rings (fig. 2). It is interesting that no grave contained both a bracelet and a ring (see fig. 6, which illustrates the distribution of ornamentation by grave and excavation area). If prestige can be identified based on variation in the number of grave goods associated with a burial,[70] we assume that the burials with metal artifacts represent the highest-ranking individuals in the cemetery excavation, simply because the production of metal and metal objects was more labor-intensive and "knowledge-laden" than bead production. According, there is no ques-

70. L. R. Binford, "Mortuary Practices: Their Study and Potential," in *Approaches to the Social Dimensions of Mortuary Practices* (ed. J. A. Brown; Memoirs of the Society for American Archaeology 25; Washington, D.C.: The Society for American Archaeology, 1971) 6–29; R. Chapman, I. Kinnes, and K. Randsborg, *The Archaeology of Death* (London: Cambridge University Press, 1981); N. A. Rothschild, "Mortuary Behaviour and Social Organisation at Indian Knoll and Dickson Mounds," *American Antiquity* 44 (1979) 658–79.

Fig. 8. Overview of Grave 93.

tion that Grave 92 (fig. 8) represents the highest-ranking individual (a mature female) excavated in the cemetery. The woman was buried with 3 bracelets (2 copper, 1 iron), 28 beads (3 were on a string), and a scarab, a garland of 5 pomegranates, a large wooden bowl fragment, and a spindle whorl. However, ascribing the term "highest ranking" is purely relative here. If we examine the distribution of metal ornaments and scarabs by age and sex (fig. 7), as we did the distribution of beads, it is clear that ornamentation represents a female burial tradition at the WFD 40 Cemetery rather than a male one. In fact, out of a total of 80 human burials, only 5 could definitely be identified as male. Of the 3 adult male graves, Grave 25 had 2 beads and Grave 31 had 1 bead. This conforms to contemporary Bedouin male practices, where an individual male will often wear a single bead on a string that functions as a charm or

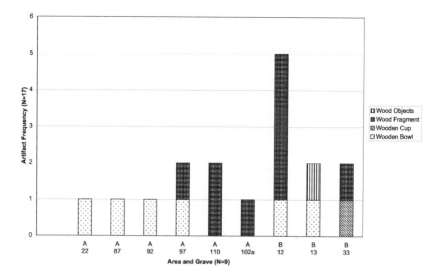

Fig. 9. Histogram: wood artifacts (indeterminate objects, bowls, cups) by area and grave.

totem to protect him. As noted above, the lack of evidence for clearly identifiable preciosities in the total cemetery excavation sample (N = 62 graves and 80 individuals) argues against using the metal ornaments (made of locally available copper and simple iron artifacts) as strict indicators or highly significant symbols of wealth.

The Distribution of Wood Artifacts

One of the biggest surprises in the WFD 40 Cemetery excavations was the complete absence of pottery vessels in the grave assemblage. While little systematic research has been done on Bedouin burial practices,[71] ethnographic collections[72] demonstrate the importance of "unbreakable" wooden vessels that could be easily packed and would survive camel and donkey journeys across the desert. The assumption made here is that the inclusion of wooden artifacts (mostly bowls and cups) is a material correlate of a nomadic community interred in the WFD 40 Cemetery. This is not to say that the

71. Cf. J. Ben-David, *Ja'baliya: A Bedouin Tribe in the Shadow of the Monastery* (Jerusalem: Cana, 1981) [Hebrew]; Lancaster, *The Rwala Bedouin Today*; A. Marx, *Bedouin of the Negev* (Manchester: Manchester University Press, 1967); Musil, *Manners and Customs of the Rwala Bedouin.*

72. Levy, personal observation; Negev Museum and Joe Alon Bedouin Museum ethnographic collections.

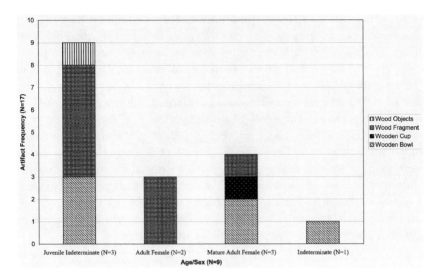

Fig. 10. Histogram: wood artifacts (bowls, fragments, indeterminate objects) by age and sex.

Iron Age nomads who were buried in the cemetery did not use pottery as part of their material culture. Frank Hole[73] and others[74] have shown that prehistoric and historic Bedouin used pottery vessels obtained from trade with sedentary societies. The ubiquitous distribution of black Gaza ware pottery sherds associated with historic Bedouin sites in Israel's Negev desert is proof of this.[75] Today, plastic bottles, jerry cans, and other readily available vessels are used by Bedouin across the Middle East. The point, however, is that pottery, plastic, and metal jerry cans are obtained on an ad hoc basis from the "outside world"[76] and do not have the same meaning that carefully burnished and curated "nomad-made" wooden vessels have. As shown in fig. 9, a total of 9 individuals were found with objects made from wood, including unidentifiable objects, miscellaneous fragments, bowl fragments, and complete cups. These were probably highly personal objects and were mostly associated with females (see fig. 10).

Finally, what preliminary remarks can be made about the social organization of the population excavated in the WFD Cemetery? The majority of

73. F. Hole, "Pastoral Nomadism in Western Iran," *Explorations in Ethnoarchaeology* (ed. R. A. Gould; Albuquerque: University of New Mexico Press, 1978) 192–218.

74. R. Cribb, *Nomads in Archaeology* (Cambridge: Cambridge University Press, 1991).

75. Levy, personal observation.

76. Khazanov, *Nomads and the Outside World.*

graves excavated in 1997 were undisturbed. This was inferred from the fact that capstones on these graves were sealed with a mud plaster before being in-filled. Thus, while there may be more than 3,000 unexcavated graves in the cemetery, our sample is as large as many carefully excavated mortuary sites in the archaeological record.[77] From the discussion above, it seems that there was no rigid social hierarchy in which positions of status were inherited, as might be expected in a non-village sedentary society. In the relatively small sample of graves (N = 62), women were given more gifts and attention in the burial ritual than men. The location of small children in their own graves near adults or included as secondary burials with adults suggests that the clusters of graves (fig. 2) observed in the cemetery represent family clusters. Only when a more statistically based analysis of the WFD 40 Cemetery's hu-man, burial facility, and grave good inventory is made will it be possible to elaborate more on the social dimensions of this community.

Conclusion

The identification of ethnicity in the archaeological record is a method-ological problem fraught with difficulties. Pre-1945 German abuse of pre-history and archaeology in the name of National Socialist expansion of the German territorial state using the theories of G. Kossina has made archaeol-ogists shy away from issues related to identifying ethnic groups archaeologi-cally.[78] The quest for a purely scientific archaeology with generalized "laws of human behavior" was proposed by the "New Archaeology" in the 1960s[79] and resulted in an abandonment of interest in the role of historical processes on culture change. Perhaps the most important critique made by "Post-Processual Archaeology" in the mid-1980s of their "Processual" predecessors was the cry to reintegrate the role of history in archaeological analyses of the past.[80] It is fair to say that epigraphic and textual data are an integral part of the archaeological record. To ignore these historical sources is tantamount to throwing away the context in which archaeological phenomena were formed. Bearing in mind the mistakes of the past as highlighted in Bettina Arnold's study of National Socialist Germany, archaeologists today are challenged by the myriad of archaeological, historical, and environmental data at their dis-posal to explain what happened in the past. The "Post-Processual" critique

77. Chapman, Kinnes, and Randsborg, *Archaeology of Death.*
78. B. Arnold, "Past as Propaganda: Totalitarian Archaeology in Nazi Germany," *Antiquity* 64/244 (1990) 464–78.
79. P. J. Watson, S. A. LeBlanc, and C. L. Redman, *Explanation in Archeology: An Explicitly Scientific Approach* (New York: Columbia University Press, 1971).
80. I. Hodder (ed.), *Symbolic and Structural Archaeology* (Cambridge: Cambridge University Press, 1982).

has also made inroads into the archaeology of the "Holy Land" as character-ized in the works of Neil Silberman.[81] In these works, archaeology and in particular biblical archaeology are deconstructed using the methodology of literary criticism to show the political biases of the practitioners. Even the harshest critics of biblical archaeology have not suggested that archaeologists abandon the search for the ethnic groups that pepper the biblical and extra-biblical textual sources. It is essential to confront the issue of ethnicity as re-vealed in these sources if we are to understand the history and archaeology of the southern Levant. However, scholars should make every effort not to re-peat the errors of earlier archaeologists alluded to above. It is in this spirit that we have begun to probe the identity of the Iron Age people buried in the Wadi Fidan 40 Cemetery.

Most archaeologists and ancient historians who have carried out field work in the region of Edom have had little problem in suggesting that dur-ing the Late Bronze/Early Iron Age, Edom was home to the Shasu nomads.[82] However, until the recent excavations at the Wadi Fidan 40 Cemetery, there had been no site excavated in Edom that could definitely be ascribed to the Shasu.

From this recent research in the Jabal Hamrat Fidan, we have for the first time begun the task of relating the historical and textual evidence for the Early Iron Age of Edom with the archaeological record. The exact identity of the population of the Wadi Fidan 40 Cemetery as part of the "Shasu" may never be definitively established, but the archaeological and textual/historical linkages, as outlined above, suggest that in this case the archaeological record supports the biblical and historical/textual evidence.

81. N. A. Silberman, *Digging for God and Country: Exploration, Archeology, and the Se-cret Struggle for the Holy Land, 1799–1917* (New York: Knopf, 1982); idem, *Between Past and Present: Archaeology, Ideology, and Nationalism in the Modern Middle East* (New York: Holt, 1989).

82. Bienkowski and van der Steen, "Tribes, Trade, and Towns"; D. Hopkins, "Pasto-ralists in Late Bronze Age Palestine: Which Way Did They Go?" *BA* 56 (1993) 200–211; Kitchen, "Egyptian Evidence on Ancient Jordan"; Knauf, "The Cultural Impact of Second-ary State Formation: The Cases of the Edomites and the Moabites," in *Early Edom and Moab: The Beginning of the Iron Age in Southern Jordan* (ed. P. Bienkowski; Sheffield: Collis, 1992) 47–54; LaBianca and Younker, "The Kingdoms of Ammon, Moab and Edom"; Levy, Adams, and Shafiq, "The Jabal Hamrat Fidan Project."

Chapter 7

The Temple Mount:
The Afterlife of a Biblical Phrase

David Goodblatt

One of the most memorable phrases to emerge from the Six Day War, at least for Israelis, was the three-word report sent by then paratroop commander Colonel Motta Gur to the head of the Central Command, General Uzi Narkiss: הר הבית בידינו 'The temple mount is in our hands'. The Hebrew words הר הבית, literally 'the mountain of the House', refer today to the artificial platform created by Herod to support his expansion and reconstruction of the temple to the God of Israel in Jerusalem. Holding in the landfill that helps form the platform are massive retaining walls, part of which is the famous Western (or "Wailing") Wall. After the Arab conquest of Palestine, several shrines and mosques were constructed on the platform, including the Dome of the Rock (commonly called the Mosque of Omar) and the Al-Aqsa Mosque. Muslims refer to the platform as the *haram al-sharif* 'the noble sanctuary'. But all of this is "recent history." The term הר הבית in fact precedes Herod and his construction project by centuries. In earlier times the phrase *temple mount* would have referred to the natural hilltop on which more-ancient temples had stood. But once the original landscape was transformed, the artificial platform became the "temple mount."[1] The changes in the

---

Author's note: For the past decade and more, I have been privileged to have David Noel Freedman as a colleague and office neighbor. He has taught me much, both formally and informally. The formal learning resulted from hearing him lecture and reading his publications. The informal learning came from observing the example he set of hard work, openness to other viewpoints, and generosity to all. I am happy to make this modest contribution to a volume honoring him and hope he will forgive me for at least partially intruding on his territory.

1. For an overview of the Herodian construction, see D. Bahat, "The temple mount and Its Environs," in the article "Jerusalem," in *NEAEHL* 2.736–44. For dissenting views on the precise limits of the area called הר הבית, see the articles by Kaufman and Jacobson in n. 13 below. On pre-Herodian extensions of the natural hilltop, see B. Mazar, "The

physical landscape aside, in this paper I will focus on the history of the phrase
הר הבית.[2]

The term הר הבית goes back to the Bible. But while common in Modern
Hebrew, it is quite rare in Biblical Hebrew. In fact, the phrase occurs in only
a single verse—although this verse appears twice in the Bible. The passage in
question is Mic 3:12. As is well known, this passage is explicitly quoted in Jer
26:18. By explicit I mean that the text in Jeremiah quotes the verse in the
name of Micah. Closely related to הר הבית is another term that also occurs
in only a single verse, but again one appearing twice in the Bible. This is the
phrase הר בית יהוה 'the mountain of the House of Yahweh', in Mic 4:1 = Isa
2:2. The honoree of this volume recently produced, in collaboration with
Francis I. Andersen, a commentary on Micah. Consequently, we can benefit
from his treatment of some of the issues concerning the verses in which these
unique biblical terms appear.

Mic 3:12 in the Masoretic Text as translated by Freedman and Andersen
reads,

> Therefore, on account of you
> Zion will be plowed like a field
> And Jerusalem will become rubbish heaps
> And the mountain of the house [הר הבית] high places of the forest.[3]

Temple Mount," *Biblical Archaeology Today: Proceedings of the International Congress of Biblical Archaeology—Jerusalem, April 1984* (Jerusalem: Israel Exploration Society, Israel Academy of Sciences and Humanities in cooperation with the American Schools of Oriental Research, 1985) 463–68.

2. After this essay was completed, I discovered that many of its findings were already observed by Yaron Z. Eliav in an unpublished doctoral dissertation submitted to Hebrew University in 5759/1998–99, *A "Mount without a Temple"—The Temple Mount from 70 CE to the Mid–Fifth Century: Reality and Idea*. I have not seen the dissertation, but portions of it are now appearing in print. See idem, " 'Interpretive Citation' in the Epistle of *Barnabas* and the Early Christian Attitude towards the Temple Mount," in *The Interpretation of Scripture in Early Judaism and Christianity: Studies in Language and Tradition* (ed. Craig A. Evans; JSPSup 33 / Studies in Scripture in Early Judaism and Christianity 7; Sheffield: Sheffield Academic Press, 2000) 353–62; idem, "*Har habbayit kěměqom pulhan ukěmerkaz politi bayahadut uvěnasrut: Iyyun mehadash*," in *Ribbonut ha'el věha'adam: Qědushah umerkaziyut polit běhar habbayit* (ed. Yizhaq Riter; Jerusalem: Makhon Yerushalayim Lěheqer Yisra'el and Merkaz Teddy Kolak Lěmehqare Yerushalayim, 2001) 25–56; idem, "The Temple Mount in Jewish Liturgy: Re-examination of the Historical Backround," in *Aboda and Ibada* (ed. Seth Ward et al.; forthcoming). As will be noted below, Eliav and I differ in the interpretation of some of the data and in the contextualizing of the conclusions. Moreover, the published selections from the dissertation do not include all of the documentation that appears in the dissertation or in this essay.

3. Francis I. Andersen and David Noel Freedman, *Micah: A New Translation with Introduction and Commentary* (AB 24E; New York: Doubleday, 2000) 379 with 385 for the translation 'high places'.

They explain that "mountain" is a "catchword" connecting this passage with the oracle beginning in the next verse, Mic 4:1. There "the phrase is complete—'the mountain of the house of Yahweh.'"[4] In other words, הר הבית is an abbreviation for הר בית יהוה, 'the house' in question being 'Yahweh's house'. And 'the house of Yahweh' refers to the temple of Yahweh.[5] The 'mountain' on which the temple of Yahweh stood is identified as Mount Zion in Jerusalem. This is implicit in the parallelism of Zion, Jerusalem, and 'the mountain of the house' in Mic 3:12. Micah 4 has the same parallelism between "the mountain of the House of Yahweh" in v. 1 and the pair "Zion/ Jerusalem" in v. 2. The result is a chiastic structure:

Zion/Jerusalem	הר הבית (3:12)
הר בית יהוה	Zion/Jerusalem (4:1–2)

That Mount Zion was the site of the temple of Yahweh in Jerusalem is often stated in the biblical books.[6]

For the purposes of this study, we need not resolve the issue of the authorship of Mic 4:1–5//Isa 2:1–5.[7] However, the fact that Mic 3:12 is the only biblical text that echoes the phrase הר בית יהוה should be noted. This does not prove that the author of the later verse also wrote the end-of-days oracle in Isaiah and Micah. He could well have been influenced by a preexistent text. At the same time the occurrence of הר הבית in Mic 3:12 may limit how late we can date these parallel passages. It is no longer a matter of just Mic 4:1–5//Isa 2:1–5 being a postexilic addition, as many would have it. Since Mic 3:12 and Jer 26:18 seem to reflect the phraseology of the end-of-days oracle, they would have to be dated later still. This strikes me as improbable.

However we resolve the source-critical issues, the textual question is more important for the present investigation. Even if we conclude that the reading in the Masoretic Text is original, variants in the ancient translations can be relevant for the afterlife of the text in later Jewish literature.[8] I begin with the

---

4. Ibid., 385, and compare 404. On the longer phrase, see the comments on p. 402.

5. See Carol Meyers, "Temple, Jerusalem," *ABD* 6.352.

6. See, for example, Isa 8:18; Joel 4:17; and Ps 20:3. For a brief and convenient survey, see W. Harold Mare, "Zion (Place)," *ABD* 6.1096–97; and Jon D. Levenson, "Zion Traditions," *ABD* 6.1098–1102.

7. On the relationship between these parallel passages, see the discussion in Andersen and Freedman, *Micah*, 413–27.

8. I have consulted the standard editions of the versions and M. Goshen-Gottstein (ed.), *The Syropalestinian Version, Part I: Pentateuch and Prophets* (Jerusalem: Magnes, 1973).

Hebrew evidence. So far as I have seen, the only one of the four verses (Mic 3:12 and 4:1 and their parallels in Jeremiah and Isaiah) to appear in a Qumran manuscript is Isa 2:2. Both 1QIsaᵃ and 4QIsaᵉ have the same reading as the Masoretic Text. Both the Peshiṭta and *Targum Jonathan* agree with the Masoretic Text in all four verses, though the latter adds the word מקדשא in each case. That is, the Targum turns "the house" (Mic 3:12//Jer 26:18) and "house of" (Mic 4:1//Isa 2:2) into "house of holiness," or "sanctuary, temple." When we come to the Septuagint and the Vulgate, the evidence is mixed. The former goes it own way with the Micah/Isaiah parallel; the latter deviates in Mic 3:12, though not in the parallel in Jeremiah. The details follow.

The Septuagint of Mic 3:12//Jer 33:18 conforms to the Masoretic Text: τὸ ὄρος τοῦ οἴκου. But in Mic 4:1 it has τὸ ὄρος τοῦ κυρίου 'the mountain of the Lord'. That is, it leaves out the word 'house'. In Isa 2:2 the Septuagint has τὸ ὄρος κυρίου καὶ ὁ οἶκος τοῦ θεοῦ 'the mountain of [the] Lord and the house of the God'. As many scholars observe, the latter reading seems clumsy. Was "the house of the God" added to bring the text more into line with the Masoretic Text? The "Syropalestinian" Aramaic text of Mic 4:1, the only one of our four passages extant in this version, agrees with the briefer Septuagint: טורה דמרא 'the mountain of the Lord'. The Vulgate agrees with the Masoretic Text in Mic 4:12 and Isa 2:2: *mons domus Domini*. And the same is true in Jer 26:18, where it has *mons domus*. But in Mic 3:12 the Vulgate has *mons templi*. This may not represent a divergent text. Instead the translator may simply have wished to resolve the ambiguity of the Hebrew 'house' just as the authors of the Targum did by adding מקדשא to the latter word. The standard English translation of הר הבית does the same thing: '*temple* mount' rather than 'mountain of the house'. For our purposes the important point is the existence of the latter phrase—that is, a literal translation of הר הבית, in the Septuagint and Peshiṭta (Mic 3:12 and Jer 26[LXX 33]:18 in both) as well as in the Vulgate (Mic 3:12).

The upshot of the survey of ancient translations is that the phrase "temple mount" was available to ancient readers/hearers of the Bible who did not know Hebrew. So it could have become part of the biblically influenced vocabulary of Greek- or Latin-speaking Jews, for example, even if it was not idiomatic in their native language. However, it did not become part of that vocabulary. On the basis of the evidence at hand, the phrase had no reverberation in Jewish literature composed in these languages. The locution "mountain of the house" never appears in all the writings of Philo, of Josephus, or in the New Testament.[9] Since the phrase is so rare in Biblical Hebrew—in

---

9. For Philo, see P. Borgen, K. Fuglseth, and R. Skarsten, *The Philo Index: A Complete Word Index to the Writings of Philo of Alexandria* (Grand Rapids, Mich.: Eerdmans / Leiden: Brill, 2000) 239, s.v. οἶκος, and 247, s.v. ὄρος. None of the passages listed under the one

only the one verse and its quotation— this does not surprise us. And the absence of "house" in the Septuagint tradition of Mic 4:1 and Isa 2:2 makes the phrase "mountain of the house" less comprehensible and truly unique for the Greek-language community. What is perhaps more striking is how rare the phrase is in extrabiblical Hebrew literature of the Second Temple period. To this we now turn.

The examination of Second Temple era Hebrew literature is complicated by the fact that some of this literature survives only in translation. And not all of the writings we might consider are securely dated. Let us begin with what survives in Hebrew (or Aramaic) and certainly dates before 70 C.E. Aside from (portions of) Ben Sira and some additional fragments from Masada and the Cairo *genizah*, what we have essentially are the nonbiblical texts found near Qumran. The latter forms a considerable corpus, numbering around six hundred manuscripts by the standard accounts. Of course, many of the manuscripts are extremely fragmentary. Still, a considerable corpus remains. Moreover, it is widely agreed that many of the texts found at Qumran are not sectarian in origin. That is, they were not all composed by the residents of Qumran and do not all reflect the special ideas of the Qumran group. This is obviously the case with the biblical manuscripts, containing texts shared by all Jews. And it is assumed to be true for many of the texts not part of the Hebrew Bible. Thus the books found at Qumran may not be a representative sampling of Second Temple literature, but they are a cross-section of what was circulating at the time.[10]

---

entry appears under the other. For Josephus, see K. H. Rengstorf, *A Complete Concordance to Flavius Josephus* (Leiden: Brill, 1979) 240–41, s.v. ὄρος, cross-checked with 182–83, s.v. οἶκος. For the New Testament, see *Concordance to the Novum Testamentum Graece of Nestle-Aland, 26th Edition and to the Greek New Testament, 3rd Edition* (ed. Institute for New Testament Textual Research and the Computer Center of Münster University with the Collaboration of H. Bachmann and W. A. Slaby; 3rd ed.; Berlin: de Gruyter, 1987) 1331–34, s.v. οἶκος; and 1375–76, s.v. ὄρος.

10. Fragments of Hebrew texts were also found at Masada. In addition to a fairly extensive section of Ben Sira, the nonbiblical manuscripts included a text known from Qumran and three parabiblical texts. None of these fragments contains anything relevant to our discussion. For the nonbiblical material aside from Ben Sira, see S. Talmon, "Hebrew Fragments from Masada," in *Masada VI: Yigael Yadin Excavations 1963–1965, Final Reports* (Jerusalem: Israel Exploration Society and the Hebrew University of Jerusalem, 1998) 98–147. For the figure of around six hundred nonbiblical manuscripts found at Qumran, see J. C. VanderKam, *The Dead Sea Scrolls Today* (Grand Rapids, Mich.: Eerdmans, 1994) 31, who counts 202 biblical manuscripts. For a listing of the total 813 manuscripts, see the "Scroll Catalogue" in G. Vermes, *The Complete Dead Sea Scrolls in English* (New York: Penguin, 1997) 601–19. Needless to say, the precise numbers are likely to change as study of the texts continues. The sectarian or nonsectarian character of individual books is to be distinguished from the question of the nature of the collection as a whole or the "library." On

With the nature of the Qumran "library" in mind, we note that the phrase *har habayit* never appears in the texts found at Qumran.[11] There are references to the temple in Jerusalem and to Zion. In 4Q522 the text "prophesies" the construction of "the house for Yahweh, God of Israel" after mentioning the capture by David of "the rock of Zion." While the text is broken, this does seem to reflect the assumption that Mount Zion was the site of the temple of Solomon and its successors. A hymn dubbed the "Apostrophe to Zion" appears in three Qumran manuscripts: 11QPsª, 4Q88 (4QPsᶠ), and 11Q6 (11QPsᵇ).[12] The "New Jerusalem" document, 11Q18, and the *Temple Scroll*, 11Q19, have descriptions of (an idealized) Jerusalem and its temple. In none of these texts does the combination of "mountain" and "house" occur. Of interest in this context is the view of Schiffman concerning the phrase עיר המקדש 'city of the sanctuary' in the *Temple Scroll*. Contrary to the common view that it refers to the city of Jerusalem, Schiffman argues that the phrase refers to the *temenos* of the temple. In Herod's temple the *temenos* was essentially coterminous with the artificial platform or "temple mount."[13] Be

---

these issues, see C. Newsom, " 'Sectually Explicit' Literature from Qumran," in *The Hebrew Bible and Its Interpreters* (ed. W. H. Propp, B. Halpern, and D. N. Freedman; Biblical and Judaic Studies from the University of California, San Diego, 1; Winona Lake, Ind.: Eisenbrauns, 1990) 167–87; D. Dimant, "The Qumran Manuscripts: Contents and Significance," in *Time to Prepare the Way in the Wilderness: Papers on the Qumran Scrolls by Fellows of the Institute for Advanced Studies of the Hebrew University, Jerusalem, 1989–90* (ed. D. Dimant and L. H. Schiffman; STDJ 16; Leiden: Brill, 1995) 23–58; eadem, "The Library of Qumran: Its Contents and Character," in *The Dead Sea Scrolls Fifty Years after Their Discovery: Proceedings of the Jerusalem Congress, July 20–25, 1997* (ed. L. H. Schiffman, E. Tov, and J. C. VanderKam; Jerusalem: Israel Exploration Society in Cooperation with The Shrine of the Book, Israel Museum, 2000) 170–76.

11. See James H. Charlesworth, *Graphic Concordance to the Dead Sea Scrolls* (Tübingen: Mohr Siebeck / Louisville: Westminster/John Knox, 1991) 61, s.v. בהר; 121–22, s.v. הבית; 152, s.v. הר; 388, s.v. מהר. There were no entries for והר on p. 189 or for להר on p. 345.

12. For recent discussions, see L. H. Schiffman, "Jerusalem in the Dead Sea Scrolls," in *The Centrality of Jerusalem: Historical Perspectives* (ed. M. Poorthuis and H. Safrai; Kampen: Kok Pharos, 1996) 87; J. H. Charlesworth, *The Dead Sea Scrolls: Hebrew, Aramaic and Greek Texts with English Translations, Vol. 4A—Pseudepigraphic and Non-Masoretic Psalms and Prayers* (Tübingen: Mohr Siebeck / Louisville: Westminster/John Knox, 1997) 201.

13. See L. H. Schiffman, "*Ir Ha-Miqdash* and Its Meaning in the Temple Scroll and Other Qumran Texts," in *Sanctity of Time and Space in Tradition and Modernity* (ed. A. Houtman, M. J. H. M. Poorthuis, and J. Schwartz; Jewish and Christian Perspective Series 1; Leiden: Brill, 1998) 95–109. On the identity of the *temenos* and the artificial platform, see idem, "Descriptions of the Jerusalem Temple in Josephus and the *Temple Scroll*," in *Historical Perspectives: From the Hasmoneans to Bar Kokhba in Light of the Dead Sea Scrolls—Proceedings of the Fourth International Symposium of the Orion Center for the Study of the Dead Sea Scrolls and Associated Literature, 27–31 January, 1999* (ed. D. Goodblatt,

that as it may, we have seen that even Qumran texts describing Zion and the Temple do not mention הר הבית.[14]

Aside from the texts found near Qumran, the only extensive example of extrabiblical, pre-70 Hebrew literature to survive in its original language is Ben Sira.[15] This book refers three times to Temple construction in Jerusalem: in the days of Solomon, Zerubbabel, and Simeon, son of Yohanan. In these three references the texts use the following terms: בית (47:13; 49:12; 50:1), מקדש (47:13), היכל (49:12; 50:1, 2) and מעון (50:2). Moreover, in describing the renovations undertaken during the high-priesthood of Simeon, at the turn of the third to the second century B.C.E., Ben Sira mentions the construction of a wall, קיר. On the basis of the Greek translation, commentators suggest that this refers to a retaining wall. But in none of these passages does the word "mountain" occur.[16] In sum, Ben Sira also never uses the phrase הר הבית.

Other pre-70 Hebrew (or Aramaic) works survive in translation. The consensus view includes in this category the books of Baruch, 1 Esdras, Tobit, Judith, *Psalms of Solomon*, and 1 Maccabees, all of which are preserved in Greek in the Septuagint. Three more books in this category, *Jubilees, Enoch*, and Pseudo-Philo, are primarily preserved in other languages.[17] Setting aside

A. Pinnick, and D. R. Schwartz: Leiden: Brill, 2001) 71, 75. As Schiffman notes on the latter page, the *Temple Scroll's temenos* would have covered the entire area of Jerusalem, not just Mount Zion. There are also claims that the term הר הבית denoted an area narrower than the entire platform created by Herod. See A. S. Kaufman, "The Term Har Habbayit," *Tarbiz* 61 (1991–92) 568 [Hebrew; English summary, p. viii]; idem, "The Shape of the Ancient Temple Mount," *Judea and Samaria Research Studies: Proceedings of the 6th Annual Meeting—1996* (Kedumim/Ariel: The College of Judea and Samaria, 1997) 111–23; D. Jacobson, "Sacred Geometry: Unlocking the Secret of the Temple Mount, Part 2," *BAR* 25 (1999) 54–63, 74. The problem with these theories is that the term "temple mount" is not attested in sources contemporary with Herod's temple. Whether the descriptions of the temple in rabbinic sources, where the term does occur, originate before 70 is debated. See below, n. 24.

14. For appearances of the name "Zion" in Qumran manuscripts, see my "Ancient Zionism? The Zion Coins of the First Revolt and Their Background," *International Rennert Guest Lecture Series* 8 (2001) 17–20.

15. Fragments of Ben Sira have been identified at Qumran as well, in 2Q18. But the extensive remnants of the Hebrew original survive in two medieval copies and in the manuscript discovered at Masada.

16. Note especially M. S. Segal, *Sefer Ben Sira Hashalem* (2nd ed.; Jerusalem: Mosad Bialik, 1971–72) 343, ad 50:2. Segal writes that the Hebrew קיר "apparently refers to a wall around the temple mount (הר הבית)." But, as noted above, the latter phrase does not appear in the text of Ben Sira. Agreeing that the קיר was a retaining wall are P. Skehan and A. Di Lella, *The Wisdom of Ben Sira* (AB 39; New York: Doubleday, 1987) 548 ad 50:2ab.

17. *Jubilees* and *Enoch* are preserved in Ethiopic, Pseudo-Philo in Latin. The Hebrew or Aramaic fragments of Tobit, *Enoch*, and *Jubilees* found at Qumran were included in the

1 Maccabees, which will be treated separately below, none of the other books contains the phrase "mountain of the house" or anything like it.[18] In Jdt 9:13 the heroine address God in a prayer. She describes how the enemy threatens "thy covenant and thy hallowed house and the crest of Zion and the house of thy sons' possession." Commentators tend to regard the latter three substantives as all referring to the Jerusalem temple.[19] In addition to the apparent allusion to Mount Zion, one notes the Semitic phraseology of the end of the verse. But there is no reference to "the mountain of the house." *Enoch* 26 describes the topography of Jerusalem but does not name the mountains. In 91:13 and 93:17 the book of *Enoch* uses the word "house," with modifying phrases, to allude to the Jerusalem temple. However, the combination of this word with "mountain" does not appear in any of these passages.[20] The book of *Jubilees* mentions Mount Zion five times. Among the five is 1:29, which locates "the sanctuary of the Lord" there. Another of these verses, 18:13, identifies Mount Zion with the mountain of Gen 22:14, where the near-sacrifice of Isaac took place. But the phrase "mountain of the house" does not occur.[21] The *Biblical Antiquities* of Pseudo-Philo has the phrase "the height

---

survey above. *Psalms of Solomon* also exists in a Syriac version, and there are Greek fragments of *Enoch* and Latin ones of *Jubilees.*

18. See E. Hatch and H. A. Redpath, *A Concordance to the Septuagint and the Other Greek Versions of the Old Testament (Including the Apocryphal Books)* (Oxford: Clarendon, 1897) 2.1014–17, s.v. ὄρος. Compare L. T. Whitelocke, *An Analytical Concordance of the Books of the Apocrypha* (Washington, D.C.: University Press of America, 1978) 2.424–29, s.v. "house," 2.113–15, s.v. "mount, mountain"; Albert-Marie Denis, *Concordance greque des pseudépigraphes d'ancien testament* (Louvain-la-Neuve: Université Catholique de Louvain, 1987) 575–76, s.v. οἶκος; 591–92, s.v. ὄρος; idem, *Concordance latine des pseudépigraphes d'ancien testament* (Turnhout: Universitas Cathólica Louvaniensis, 1993) 181–82, s.v. *domus*; 317–18, s.v. *mons*; *The Old Testament Pseudepigrapha* (ed. J. H. Charlesworth; Garden City: Doubleday, 1983) 2.999, s.v. "Temple."

19. The translation is that of M. S. Enslin, *The Book of Judith: Greek Text with an English Translation, Commentary and Critical Notes* (Leiden: Brill, 1972) 127, who adheres more closely to the Greek than other translators do. Compare, inter alia, C. A. Moore, *Judith* (AB 40; Garden City: Doubleday, 1985) 190 and the NEB.

20. See *The Book of Enoch or 1 Enoch: A New English Edition with Commentary and Textual Notes by Matthew Black* (Leiden: Brill, 1985), commentary to chap. 26 on pp. 172–73; p. 86 for 91:13 and 93:7; and subject index, p. 463., s.v. "mountain," and 466, s.v. "Temple."

21. See *Jub.* 1:29; 4:26; 8:19; 18:13; 22:14. All five references are historical or eschatological. See my "Ancient Zionism?" 12–13. The identification of the site of the temple with the site of the near-sacrifice of Isaac also appears in Josephus, *Ant.* 1.226, called "Mount Moriah" there, 1.224. The latter mountain is identified as the site of Solomon's temple in 2 Chr 3:1.

of Zion" in 26:11, an apparent reference to Mount Zion. But this book also does not reflect any instances of an original הר הבית.[22]

This leaves 1 Maccabees. To my knowledge it is only here in all of surviving extrabiblical, pre-70 Hebrew (and Aramaic) literature that we find the phrase הר הבית. Strictly speaking, what we find is a reflex of it in the Greek version before us. This is clearly the case in 4:46 concerning stones from the profaned altar being stored ἐν τῷ ὄρει τοῦ οἴκου 'on the mountain of the house'. It is also likely that the same Hebrew phrase stands behind the Greek τὸ ὄρος τοῦ ἱεροῦ 'the mountain of the sanctuary', in 13:52 and 16:20. In these verses the translator may have decided on a less-literal translation, explaining thereby that "the house" in question was the temple.[23] As noted, the Vulgate to Mic 3:12 (*mons templi*), *Targum Jonathan* to all four relevant verses (טור בית מקדשא), and the current English translation ('*temple* mount') all follow the same approach.

We may thus assume that the phrase הר הבית appeared three times in the Hebrew original of 1 Maccabees. Considering its rarity in the books of the Hebrew Bible, this is a fairly large number. Of course, the book is concerned with the profanation and then purification and defense of the temple, so we would expect frequent reference to the temple environs. (While 2 Maccabees is, if anything, more focused on the temple, its Greek language would be less congenial to the Semitic idiom "mount of the house.") But if the three occurrences of הר הבית in 1 Maccabees seem fairly high, they are outweighed by the eight occurrences of the phrase "Mount Zion": 4:37; 4:60; 5:54; 6:48; 6:62; 7:33; 10:1; 14:27. In every case the reference is to contemporary events, not to history or eschatology. The sandwiching of the mention of "the mountain of the house" in 4:46 between the references to "Mount Zion" in 4:37 and 4:60 shows that both phrases denote the same location. It seems, then, that author of 1 Maccabees preferred "Mount Zion," which also was more common in biblical books. The relatively frequent occurrence of this geographical designation in the book of *Jubilees*, mentioned above, may also indicate the popularity of "Mount Zion" in Hasmonean times.

So even the one pre-70 book that used the phrase הר הבית preferred "Mount Zion" as the designation for the temple mount. These data do not

22. See H. Jacobson, *A Commentary on Pseudo-Philo's Liber Antiquitatem Biblicarum with Latin Text and English Translation* (2 vols.; Leiden: Brill, 1996) 41 for the Latin text, *excelso Syon*; p. 138 for the English translation; and pp. 772–73 for a commentary. The phrase appears to go back to the Masoretic Text of Jer 31:11, although the Vulgate (in 38:12) has "Mount Zion." See also Jacobson, *Pseudo-Philo*, 556–57, for the argument that the occurrence of the toponym "Zion" in 16:2 is a mistake. Jacobson (pp. 199–200) argues for a post-70 date for the book, but he admits that the scholarly consensus is before 70.

23. Contrast Eliav, "*Har habbayit kĕmĕqom pulhan*," 35, who suggests that the phrase "temple mount" in 1 Macc 13:52 and 16:20 are post-70 additions to the text.

prepare us for the picture that emerges from post-70 Hebrew literature. It is in this era that הר הבית becomes a common phrase, indeed the standard designation for the elevation on which the temple (had) stood. Let us look at the two primary tannaitic documents, the Mishnah and the Tosefta. The former almost certainly was produced in the early third century C.E. in Galilee. And, according to the consensus, the latter appeared in the same place somewhat later in the same century. Almost all scholars agree that these documents preserve older material, as in fact they claim to do. Less certain is whether they preserve pre-70 material, and if so, then how much. This question is especially acute with regard to the sections describing the temple precincts and cult. Do they preserve accounts or reminiscences of masters who actually visited the temple before 70? Even those who answer in the affirmative appear to concede that the accounts were collected and edited after 70. So I assume that what we find in the Mishnah and Tosefta represents post-70 Hebrew usage.[24]

What we find is quite striking. To begin with, the designation "Mount Zion" in effect never appears. The term does not occur at all in the Tosefta. It appears once in the Mishnah, in *'Abot* 6:8. But first, most commentators agree that chap. 6 is a late addition to a tractate that, in its present form, is already fairly late. That is, the language in this chapter does not reflect third-century—let alone pre-70— Hebrew but rather the late antique/early medieval stage of the language. Second, it is questionable whether the phrase originally appeared. The words "Mount Zion" occur only in a citation of a biblical verse, Isa 24:23. And the part of the verse that is of interest to the author of the passage is not the allusion to Jerusalem or the temple. The verse is cited because of its conclusion, "honor in the presence of His elders," to prove that honor is appropriate for the righteous. The author needed only the end of the verse for his proof text and could have easily omitted the first half, the part that mentions "Mount Zion." Indeed, he might well have done so, and the citation of the entire verse could be the work of a later copyist.

Based on the above evidence I think it legitimate to conclude that the geographical term "Mount Zion" never appears in the Mishnah or Tosefta. In fact, even the toponym "Zion" (without "Mount") is relatively rare in these documents. The term appears in 3 biblical verses quoted in the Mish-

---

24. The older view is that the descriptions of the temple and its cult in the Mishnah go back to eye witnesses. See S. Safrai, "Jerusalem and the Temple in the Tannaitic Literature of the First Generation after the Destruction of the Temple," in *Sanctity of Time,* 113–52. For a much more skeptical view, compare J. Neusner, *Judaism: The Evidence of the Mishnah* (Chicago: University of Chicago Press, 1981) 97–101, 150–53. Even if these accounts do, in part, go back earlier, the present form of the texts cannot be securely dated before the second century. For the dates of the Mishnah and Tosefta, see the relevant sections of G. Stemberger, *Introduction to the Talmud and Midrash* (2nd ed.; trans. and ed. M. Bockmuehl; Edinburgh: T. & T. Clark, 1996).

nah and in 9 quoted in the Tosefta. Outside of these verse citations, "Zion" occurs in a single passage, appearing in parallel versions in each document. And in this appearance it is an element in a personal or family name.[25] In any case, my focus is on the phrase for the elevation on which the temple stood, namely, "Mount Zion." In contrast to the absence of this term in the Mishnah and Tosefta, the alternative הר הבית is quite common. It appears 25 times in 19 passages in the Mishnah and 30 times in 21 passages in the Tosefta.[26] Clearly in tannaitic Hebrew הר הבית has become the standard designation for the elevation on which the temple (once) stood.

Modern Hebrew usage, then, in which הר הבית is the common term for the temple platform, originated in Middle Hebrew. Another development probably reinforced this usage. In Byzantine times the name "Mount Zion" began to be used for a hill in the southwestern quadrant of old Jerusalem.[27] The "migration" of this name to a different locale left הר הבית unopposed, as it were, as the name for the eastern hill. At the same time, it could also be that the post-70 popularity of הר הבית made "Mount Zion" available for transference and application to a different location. This is especially likely in view of the frequency of the phrase הר הבית and the absence of the toponym "Mount Zion" in second/third-century tannaitic literature, as detailed above. Be that as it may, the main conclusion is clear. While the term הר הבית has biblical roots, its usage as the common designation for the temple mount/platform is postbiblical, indeed, post–Second Temple. And this would not be the only instance in which the modern language has followed Middle Hebrew rather than Biblical Hebrew.[28]

---

25. See my "Ancient Zionism," 31–33. The data are drawn from the Bar-Ilan Responsa Project. The passage not quoting the Bible is in *m.* ʿ*Ed.* 8:7 // *t.* ʿ*Ed.* 3.4.

26. Goodblatt, "Ancient Zionism," 34.

27. See Mare, "Zion," *ABD* 6.1097.

28. For speculation about why Middle Hebrew may have favored הר הבית over "Mount Zion," see my "Ancient Zionism," 28–29, 34–35. For a different interpretation, see Eliav, "*Har habbayit kĕmĕqom pulhan.*" He suggests that the destruction of the Temple led Jews to construe the now empty platform as a holy site. But this does not explain why the phrase "temple mount" was preferred over the toponym "Mount Zion," with its much more extensive biblical pedigree. For the influence of Middle Hebrew on the modern language, the work of A. Bendavid, *Biblical Hebrew and Mishnaic Hebrew* (2 vols.; Tel-Aviv: Dvir, 1967–71) is still useful. For a broader perspective, see A. Sáenz-Badillos, *A History of the Hebrew Language* (trans. J. Elwolde; Cambridge: Cambridge University Press, 1993) 272–76.

Index of Authors

Index of Scripture

New Testament

Deuterocanonical and Pseudepigraphical Works